Young Andrew Jackson in the Carolinas

A Revolutionary Boy

Jennifer Hunsicker ★ Illustrations by Teresa Wiles

Charleston   London

THE
History
PRESS

Published by The History Press
Charleston, SC 29403
www.historypress.net

Copyright © 2014 by Jennifer Hunsicker
All rights reserved

First published 2014

Manufactured in the United States

ISBN 978.1.62619.359.8

Library of Congress CIP data applied for.

Contents

Contents

Acknowledgements

I would like to thank The History Press and everyone there who worked on turning the beginning manuscript into this final printed book. Thanks to Teresa Wiles, whose illustrations brought many scenes so vividly to life. I would like to thank the Museum of the Waxhaws and the local community for their friendliness and helpfulness during my research trip there in 2011, as well as the staff of Andrew Jackson State Park. Many thanks to Bill Maddox and Jennifer Kirk of Mansker's Station in Goodlettsville, Tennessee, and to Terry Palmer for sharing their knowledge of this time period. Thanks to my writing buddies Karen and Connie for their encouragement and support and to Katie for being my cheerleader. Many, many thanks to my family for their patience during the time my writing took me away. I cannot forget where this manuscript began, Spalding University—thank you. And I have to mention that I would not have been able to complete this manuscript without the print resources of Nashville Public Library, as well as its interlibrary loan department. Thanks also to the Society of Children's Book Writers and Illustrators for the educational opportunities offered through workshops, conferences and listservs over the years.

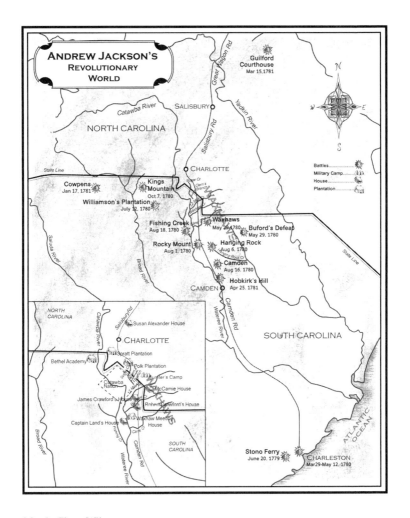

Map by Teresa Wiles.

Chapter 1
Who Was Andrew Jackson?

A ndrew Jackson grew up to become the seventh president of the United States of America, serving from 1829 to 1837. He became a great leader, but many people did not agree with his decisions. Known as the "People's President," some people continued to vote for him for president as many as fifteen years after his death.

Young Andy had a rough start in this world. His parents had only immigrated to this country from Ireland a couple of years earlier when tragedy struck. His father died just a few weeks before Andy was born in 1767. Growing up during the Revolutionary War gave him the basis of the military and leadership skills he would carry and build on for the rest of his life. This war took away his mother and his two brothers. He lived with the Crawfords, his mother's people, after her death. There, he found shelter, family connections and foundational skills on which to build a career.

He had a temper and enjoyed having fun and being a bit of a prankster before settling down to a law and military career. This was definitely not the ministerial career his mother had hoped for him. Later, he was involved in scandals and known to fight in duels.

The Revolutionary War was prominent in developing his leadership skills. He served as a messenger during the war at age thirteen, watching many family members and friends fall in battle. Before that, the Revolutionary War had not touched the backcountry of the Carolinas much until the British tried to take Charleston. Charleston at this time was the largest and wealthiest city in the South. It was also a port city, which made it a tactical draw. The British slowly moved inward, and the Scotch-Irish settlers were not going to take it. They fought back. During the skirmishes in the backcountry, Jackson learned to hate the British. They not only left him with physical scars, but it was also because of them that he lost his family. He would carry this hatred the rest of his life.

What made Jackson become the man he did? His youth and his Scotch-Irish heritage had much to do with that.

Chapter 2

Andy's Parents Journey to America

The ocean lay before them and the shores of Ulster, Ireland, behind them. Their hearts waved goodbye to the life they had known. With each splash of a wave and wisp of the wind bellowing the sails, they headed out to open sea and on to a new life in America.

In April 1765, the parents of future president Andrew Jackson watched the shores of Ireland disappear from their view on the ship. Andrew and Betty Jackson must have been filled with excitement, as well as a little bit of nervousness, as they began this adventure toward their new life. They brought their two young sons with them: Hugh, two years old, and Robert, only five months old. Their son Andy would not be born for another two years. Approximately one hundred other passengers chose to make this journey as well. But why? Why did they decide to make this long, nearly two-month voyage into the unknown? This was, after all, a voyage they might not survive, that could cause disease and possible starvation if the food ran out, that would provide uncomfortable bedding and few opportunities, if any, for bathing or other hygiene.

They were escaping to the possibility of a better life. Life in Ireland had been hard. No matter how hard they worked, they never seemed to get ahead. South Carolina began offering free

land to settlers in 1761, which attracted many immigrants. Most of these Irish immigrants were Presbyterian. Known as Scotch-Irish Americans, earlier generations of them had left Scotland for Ireland in the seventeenth century. They began immigrating to America around 1720. The free land in South Carolina meant a chance at bettering their lives. Some came from extreme poverty. Others came from middle-income families. Either way, this was a chance to change what was assured if they stayed. In Ireland, even prosperous families who grew the flax for the linen or were engaged in the manufacturing of linen were tenants of English nobles. Rent was due once or twice per year on their tenant lease. There was nothing to pass on to future generations.

Carolina land was heavily forested, with enough pastureland for grazing cattle as well as vines and cane for them to feed upon. Ulster families relied on dairy products: milk, butter and buttermilk. In America, they could brand their cattle and let them wander in the woods rather than just being able to keep one cow in a fenced yard, as in Ireland.

In the Waxhaws, their destination in America, there was a Presbyterian church with a minister trained at the University of Glasgow. If there was a church in the community, there was some sort of community leadership and rules to provide order. The elders of the church monitored community conduct and settled disputes.

Betty Jackson was a fiery, petite, blue-eyed redhead full of energy. She was young, only in her mid-twenties, and loved to talk. She was tough, too. She had to be to endure life on a ship that came to America and the trials of colonial life on the frontier. Betty, an expert spinner, came from a family steeped in the linen trade. They spun flax from the fields into linen thread, which was woven into cloth. Her family was from the County Antrim near Carrickfergus, which was located north of Belfast on the coast of Ulster.

We know very little of Andrew's side of the family. Andrew hoped to become a landowner someday. He turned down a weaving apprenticeship to become a tenant farmer. His father, Hugh, was a linen weaver and merchant in Carrickfergus. According to Andrew Jr., later in life, his parents were well off enough to buy their own passage to America, as well as land.

Andrew Sr. had three brothers: Hugh Jr., Samuel and Robert. Hugh served in His Majesty's Forty-ninth Regiment of Foot. During his service, he traveled from Ireland through Virginia in America and Quebec and Montreal in Canada. He fought Cherokee Indians in the Waxhaws in North and South Carolina in America and hunted with the Catawba Indians. Most importantly, though, Hugh Jackson passed on his knowledge of America to Andrew Jackson; his wife, Elizabeth; and nineteen other Irish families. He convinced them of the opportunities awaiting them in America, especially land of their own. Unfortunately, Hugh's wife did not want to leave Ireland, and all but two other families besides the Jacksons decided to stay in Ireland with the familiar rather than reach for the possibility of the unknown.

Betty and Andrew headed for the Waxhaws on the border between North and South Carolina. This area today is just south of Charlotte, North Carolina, and into Lancaster, South Carolina, with the Catawba River to the west and Monroe, North Carolina, to the east. Betty, the youngest of six sisters, already had family in the area. At least three of the Hutchinson sisters were already there. In the 1760s, all six of them, along with their husbands, settled in this area. Many other immigrants in the area were also from County Antrim in Ireland. It was common for Irish families to immigrate in clan-like units. They knew what they would find, who they would meet and what kind of support system they would have there.

It is likely that Betty's sister Jane, the sister she was the closest to, and her husband, James Crawford, and their children were with them on this voyage. The Crawford children ranged in age from four to ten. James was a quiet, hardworking man. Jane and Betty were very close. Jane may have had health problems, as she was described as an invalid a few years later. Another sister, Grace, may have been on the boat with them as well. Andrew's brother Samuel, a world sailor, may have served on their boat for the long voyage.

There is some confusion as to whether Betty and Andrew arrived in America at the Philadelphia port or the Charleston port. Either way, they would travel the Great Wagon Road, a long dirt road that ran from Pennsylvania through Virginia to the Carolinas. This was the main road into the Carolina backcountry.

A Revolutionary Boy

The boat arrived in America in May 1765 during the heat of summer. If they arrived at the Charleston port, they experienced stifling humidity, a very different climate from what they were used to in Ireland. As a sailor who had been here before, Samuel would have been able to tell them how to get provisions and where to stay along their journey to the Waxhaws. Samuel may not have been able to accompany them on their journey, though. His work may have been back on ship. They knew no one else in Charleston. They stepped off the boat into an unfamiliar land with the adventure of a new life before them. Dripping with sweat and in need of baths, they prepared for their trip. Along with other immigrant settlers, they obtained supplies, horses and a wagon to travel the Great Wagon Road.

Leaving the bustle of a big city like Charleston, they saw the contrast of their villages in Ireland to the Carolina country they entered. In Ulster, the villages were about five miles apart, but in the wooded Carolinas, there may be between ten and twenty miles between towns. In between, there was nothing but nature. There was nothing but birds in the trees, fish in the rivers, a few other critters scurrying about and scattered log homes and taverns along the way. While many frontier settlers opened their homes to travelers, a few places along the way charged fees. These were taverns. They offered drink, meals and/or a place to stay, but they charged money for it. This would be like staying in a motel today, but in the Jacksons' time, accommodations were not quite as comfortable.

The roads then were not as developed as they are today. These were dirt roads or sometimes just paths. They were muddy, with potholes and rocks and gravel, which made for a bumpy ride by wagon. Outside Charleston, they traveled through swampy land. They passed tall cypress trees draped with Spanish moss, palmettos with sword-like leaves and occasionally flocks of green and gold parakeets. There were many mosquitoes in this hot climate. These new settlers were told it would take a year or two before they grew accustomed to this climate and could resist illnesses like malaria. It was not known at the time, but mosquitoes transmitted malaria to humans.

Along the Great Wagon Road, they only saw one other town, Camden. Over one hundred miles and two and a half days from

Charleston, Camden was a fairly new and growing settlement. This would be their trading town for any goods they wanted to sell in the future. They soon found out about another market town, Salisbury, located north of the Waxhaw settlement, which would also be a place they used for trade. As they traveled north of Camden, the swamps and cypress trees disappeared. Dense woods took their place, with only occasional patches of rock and grass. The sandy soil of the swamps became a reddish clay, which was very important to the Catawba Indians. The Great Wagon Road became the Camden Road or the Catawba Path, a trading path created by the Catawba Indians as they traveled back and forth from their villages for trade. This was still the Great Wagon Road, but the name changed to Camden Road, Salisbury Road, Camden-Salisbury Road, Salisbury-Camden Road or Charleston-Salisbury Road, depending on which direction you traveled. Remember, the Great Wagon Road ran from Pennsylvania through the Carolinas. This road name change is like Main Street through a small town. If you follow it on the map, it may be known as another name or even multiple names even though it is the same road.

One more day and Betty, Andrew and their family were in their dreamed-of Waxhaws.

Chapter 3
The Waxhaws

The large, barnlike Waxhaw Meeting House in the center of town greeted them. The gushing Catawba River separated the settlement on the east and the Catawba Nation to the west. They were in pine tree country. All different kinds of pines mixed with a variety of other trees such as oak and hickory in this heavily wooded land. There were pine trees with needles that stretched down to the ground, pine trees with needles that stretched out to the sides and pine trees with needles that reached up to the sky. There were short trees and tall trees and in-between trees. These pines seemed to represent the people of the community, where church was the nucleus of this primarily Presbyterian settlement. Their homes extended within a radius of ten to fifteen miles from the Waxhaw Meeting House. Fields and forests spread between them. Unlike the suburbs of today, where a neighbor is right next door, they were a community but with distance being a way of life. By 1770, approximately 120 families or six to seven hundred people lived here. A bit farther north, in Hillsborough, North Carolina, one thousand settler wagons were recorded passing through during 1765, the year Betty and Andrew arrived.

Why was a church so important? It meant civilization, grounding and governance had already been established. The church represented decency and orderliness. Within the church, elders monitored the congregation's conduct while addressing complaints about behavior and settling disputes. The Waxhaw Meeting House had a minister, William Richardson, who had trained at the University of Glasgow, an important qualification to these Scotch-Irish settlers. Sunday worship was a regular part of their lives, but the church was a part of daily living.

By 1768, nearly all of the Hutchinson sisters were married and settled in the Waxhaw area of the Carolinas. All but Peggy, the eldest, and Betty, the youngest, met and married their husbands after their arrival in America.

> *Margaret (Peggy) Hutchinson married George McCamie.*
> *Sarah Hutchinson married Samuel Leslie.*
> *Mary Hutchinson married John Leslie.*
> *Jennet (Jane) Hutchinson married James Crawford.*
> *Elizabeth (Betty) Hutchinson married Andrew Jackson.*
> *Grace Hutchinson married James Crow.*

James, Joseph and Robert Crawford were born in Scotch-Irish southeastern Pennsylvania. Their father was Colonel John Crawford of Ayrshire, Scotland. They arrived in the Waxhaws in 1760. This was five years before Betty and Andrew arrived. Robert and Joseph received their Waxhaw land in 1763, but Joseph died not long after that. Jane and James Crawford were married a few years earlier in Pennsylvania and settled in the Waxhaws in 1763. James received his official title to the land in 1768, though he was already living there at the same time as his brothers. If it is true that Jane and James were on the boat with Betty and Andrew, they must have traveled back to Ireland with their children for a visit and to persuade others to join them on the return voyage.

The 110-acre James Crawford farm was located along the Crawford's Branch of Waxhaw Creek. A year after Jane's arrival, Peggy and George McCamie bought a farm two and a half miles away from the Crawfords, just down the Camden-Salisbury Road. On this land, they built a cabin with a stone chimney. Mary, Sarah and their husbands lived in their respective homes within two or three miles of their sisters. Grace and James Crow settled nearby on 350 acres in 1768.

Andrew Jackson Sr. settled his family on two hundred acres situated ten miles from Jane and James Crawford. They were four miles from the Camden-Salisbury Road and eight miles from the McCamies. Here at the Ligget's Branch of Twelve Mile Creek, they were twelve miles from the church, which they visited every Sunday. They chose the Waxhaw Meeting House over the closer Sugar Creek Meeting House because Betty wanted to worship and visit with her sisters. It is likely that most, if not all, of her sisters attended here. The soil on Jackson's land was clay-like, not dark and fertile. This made digging, building and sowing crops more of a challenge. It was covered in scrub pine, hickory and oak trees. Much of the land in this area had already been taken. If Andrew thought it was more important to have fertile soil, he would have settled about twenty miles farther away. He did not. He and Betty wanted to settle near family, so here is where they stayed.

Andrew, Betty and their sons had traveled 3,500 miles to get here from Ireland. They stayed with one of Betty's sisters while Andrew cleared land and built his family a log cabin. With help from family and friends, a starter cabin could go up in a day. Well, not the entire cabin, but at least the sides, a roof and a stone chimney. These starter cabins were only one room with one fireplace and a loft. Chinking, or filling, between the logs and wooden planks to cover bare dirt floors would be added later. Furniture was built, not bought.

In Ireland, their houses were small like these settler cabins, but they were made out of stone or mud with thatched roofs. Like most new settler cabins, theirs was probably twenty-two to twenty-four feet wide and sixteen feet deep. Doors in the front and back provided entry. The clay or mud filling between the logs kept out the wind and cold. On one end of the house was a stone chimney. There were very few windows, since glass was a precious commodity. Glass meant you were established and successful. Until then, oilcloth or oiled paper might have covered the windows. This made the room dark, and the fireplace made the room smoky. After they were settled there for a while, the single room downstairs would either be divided into two rooms or a second room would be added on later

William Morris cabin, Saluda, Polk County, North Carolina, built in 1790. Though this photo is taken much later, this cabin is representative of the interior of backcountry homes during the Revolutionary War. Notice the chinking between the logs and fiddle to the side. *Library of Congress Prints and Photographs Division.*

to become the kitchen and a small bedroom. Children usually slept upstairs in the loft, where household goods were also stored. Often, especially if it were cold, the family may have slept on blankets in front of the fire, just as they would have in Ireland. There may also have been slats for rifles in the loft in case of attack on this frontier.

As families stayed longer and became more settled and prosperous, their homes might grow to two stories, be covered with clapboard and have shuttered windows. Chimneys might also be made of brick in the wealthier homes. Only a few of the wealthier homes in this period were frame houses.

Homes in the Waxhaws included several outbuildings, much like today we might have a garage or workshop outside. A

The Secrest cabin at the Museum of the Waxhaws, built before 1830, Waxhaw, North Carolina. *Photo by author.*

rectangular wooden rail fence enclosed bare ground around a cabin. Their log outbuildings may have included a smokehouse to preserve meat, a corncrib for storing crops, a chicken coop and a springhouse for keeping crocks of milk and buttermilk cold. Larger homes may have had even more specialized buildings, such as housing a forge for blacksmithing, a separate kitchen, a saddlery shop or slave quarters.

Across the river lived Indians of the Catawba Nation, the only federally recognized tribe in the state of South Carolina today. There, for more than a century as of the 1760s, their land consisted of a square tract stretching fifteen miles on either side of the Catawba River. Known as the "People of the River,"[1] they are recognized for their unglazed and unpainted distinctive pottery made from the red clay so common in this area. The color of this pottery was only achievable because of this clay and the firing process involved. The Catawba often visited the Waxhaw settlement to sell their pottery; however, they tended to keep to themselves except for trade. An

A log chicken coop. Historic Brattonsville. McConnells, South Carolina. *Photo by author.*

exception was a unique Patriot alliance during the Revolutionary War. The Catawba are still in the Waxhaws today. They continue to sell their artisan pottery, as well as other artisan pieces such as hand-woven baskets.

Chapter 4
Birth of a Future President

Snow fell on a cold day in February 1767 as Andrew Jackson Sr. lay dying. He had worked so hard to make a life for himself and his family. He was injured in a logging accident, perhaps straining himself. This was complicated by other things, not the least likely of which was exhaustion. He was only about twenty-seven years old. He did not live to see the birth of his youngest son, the future president of the United States.

These Scotch-Irish settlers were very clan-like, as well as superstitious. Once the word got out that Betty's husband had passed, neighbors and family gathered at the Jackson cabin for a typical Irish wake before transporting the body for burial. Andrew's body would have been set on a table in the middle of the main room of their home. Coins rested on his eyes and a plate of salt on his chest. The little furniture they had was rearranged for sitting around the body through the night for protection and passage into the next world. All glass, especially mirrors, was covered. Clocks were stopped, and their dial plates were covered. Light food was prepared for the evening ahead. A crackling fire stayed lit for warmth.

Family and friends surrounded Betty and the children during this time of grief. They said prayers and read from the Bible. They ate.

They chatted about everyday business, not of eternity or loss. They may have shared comforting memories of Andrew. The men may have discussed crops or business while the women shared family or community news. The house was small. Some sat on the floor. Some traveled back and forth inside and out as preparations for the next day's journey were underway. Drinking was part of their daily lives. The whiskey gourd was passed around. As the night closed in, some slept while at least one stayed up all night with the body, as was part of Irish tradition.

The next morning, everyone was ready for the journey over the ice and through the snow to the cemetery. A mule was hitched to a sled to carry the coffin, accompanied by the pallbearers. Alongside the coffin were case bottles of whiskey in a wooden box for the road. Betty moved slowly with grief and because she was just a few weeks away from giving birth to their third child. She boarded a wagon with her two young sons, Hugh, age four, and Robert, age two, leading the funeral procession of mourners. They must travel in the cold, ice and snow twelve miles to the Waxhaw Meeting House. It would not be a quick journey.

The sled struggled to get over the broken ice of the creeks that intersected the curving road, less developed than the main Camden Road, through the woods. It was a physical and tiring job in this cold to get the sled across the ice. Each time they stopped at one of the creek branches, members of the funeral procession took customary drinks of the whiskey. They traveled eight miles to Peggy and George McCamie's cabin, where they rested a bit, warmed up and received refreshments. New members joined the funeral procession as they journeyed on in the cold. Jane and James Crawford's cabin, two miles farther along, was the next stop for rest, food and drink. Inside, they passed around a jug of brandy, probably made from James Crawford's personal still. They did not stay long. Night was near, and they were still two miles away from the cemetery.

The wagons crossed Waxhaw Creek on the way to the meeting house. The sled left the road to cross at a different point. More sips of whiskey were passed around each time they crossed a creek. There were a lot of creeks. Before they knew it, night

A Revolutionary Boy

had fallen. Mourners gathered around the graveside under the stars and moonlight as the pallbearers arrived through the woods behind the cemetery with the sled. As they went behind the sled to remove the coffin, they must have gasped in surprise. It was not there! How could that be? Andrew's body was lost somewhere in the woods. Imagine Betty's disbelief and horror as she stood in the cold by her husband's graveside. The pallbearers scurried back the way they had come, shuffling through snow and crunching ice and fighting the biting cold. Snagged in the brush of the steep slope of Waxhaw Creek, they found the coffin. They quickly brought it back to the graveside, where Reverend William Richardson presided over the service.

Afterward, Betty, her boys and several guests headed back the two miles to Jane and James Crawford's cabin for the night. Betty then either stayed there or with her sister Peggy at the McCamie cabin. She did not return to her own cabin. Regardless of whether she stayed at the Crawford or the McCamie cabin, she gave birth to Andrew Jackson Jr. before sunrise on March 15, 1767. The location of his birth would not have caused much of a dispute if he had not become president of the United States. He did, however, and though the cabins were only a few miles apart, they were in two different states.

One side of Jackson's family has given statements that say he was born in North Carolina at the Peggy and George McCamie cabin. They say Betty gave birth and stayed there for three weeks. She then went on to stay with her sister Jane and her husband, James Crawford, at their home for the rest of her life. Andy's cousin Sarah Lathan, daughter of Andy's aunt Sarah Leslie, remembers that as a seven-year-old child she was called to help with the birth and went "through the fields in the night time."[2] Sarah and Samuel Leslie's home was only a half mile from the McCamies'. Betty would have wanted her sisters with her for the birth, especially after just losing her husband. Elizabeth McWhorter, her son George and Mary Cousar were all "near neighbours [sic] and present on the night of the birth of General Jackson or were there the next day."[3]

As a grown man, however, Andrew Jackson Jr. claimed that family history told him that he was born in the James Crawford cabin in

The marker for the birthplace of Andrew Jackson, Andrew Jackson State Park, South Carolina Department of Parks, Recreation & Tourism. *Photo by author.*

South Carolina. Jackson always claimed South Carolina as his birth state. The fact remains that Andy lived, worked and played along the Waxhaws' fuzzy border between North and South Carolina. He spent his youth in the Carolinas, never to return again once he left.

After Andy's birth, he was baptized in the Waxhaw Meeting House, also known as Old Waxhaw Presbyterian Church, by Reverend Richardson. Regardless of where he was born, he grew up in the James Crawford cabin. Betty never again lived in a home of her own. She did keep her two hundred acres of land until a clear title could be conveyed. In 1770, she had that property deeded to her sons, Hugh, Robert and Andrew. Andrew Jackson became a landowner at the age of three. He kept this land until 1792, though he never lived on it.

Betty knew she needed help raising her sons and living on the frontier. Her sister Jane was ill. It made sense for Betty to move in with the Crawfords. Jane and James were glad for the help in raising their own children and for Betty's help around the house. There were four Crawford children, all boys. Ranging in age from six to twelve, their names were Will, Joey, Jim and Tommy. All seven boys slept upstairs in the loft.

Betty liked to stay busy. She was hardworking and did not wish to be a burden on her brother-in-law. When Hugh, her oldest son, was six or seven, she sent him to live with her sister Peggy and husband George McCamie. With no children of their own, Hugh was a big help to them with small chores around the house. They were only about a mile down the road from Betty. Andy and Robert were so young that it seemed natural to them to walk the mile down the road to see their brother. Sometimes they visited on their way to Walkup's Mill just a bit farther down the road. Perhaps, Hugh went to the mill with them to take grain for grinding into meal for the McCamies. If the boys traveled in the other direction, they were at the home of Robert Crawford, James Crawford's brother, whom they thought of as an uncle.

Robert Crawford, more affluent than his brother James, lived in a two-story home. He also had a stronger personality, while James was the quiet one. Robert became more and more important in the area as time passed. Eventually, he became captain and then major of the local militia in the 1770s. James served under him.

Most families in this area owned guns for hunting, as well as protection if needed. Occasionally, a wildcat or wolf was spotted, but most hunting game included deer and small animals to feed their families. At an early age, boys learned about guns. Andy enjoyed a good joke, but one time, a joke by a group of older boys got the best of him. Andy was only about eight years old. He was full of spunk and tried to keep up with the older boys. A group of them overloaded a gun muzzle with a heavy charge of powder and gave it to Andy to fire. Andy did not know the gun was overloaded. The older boys waited as Andy took aim at whatever target they were using at the time. He fired a blast whose recoil sent him sprawling. It probably hurt a bit, too. Andy may have been small, but he got back up, mad as all get out.

Likely red-faced with embarrassment as well as anger, he yelled, "By God, if any of you laughs, I'll kill him."[4]

The Camden Road ran through the Waxhaw settlement. Steady traffic from both directions was varied. There were horseback riders from all classes of people. Herds of cattle headed for the beef market in Charleston thundered past, kicking up dirt. A wagon carrying goods to Camden or bringing a family to a new home was likely to lumber by. Sometimes they would stop to talk, drink or have a bite to eat. Living so close to the road meant Andy was exposed to many different types of people at an early age.

Goods traveling to Camden for sale or trade were local. Locally grown wheat was sold to Joseph Kershaw, a Camden merchant. On the east side of the Waxhaws, John Walker, an Irish immigrant, ran a country store. Goods were sold at his store as well. Walker's son, Andrew, was an expert horseman who drove many herds of their cattle on to Charleston.

On May 20, 1772, when Andy was five, he and his brothers Hugh and Robert, along with their cousins, probably saw a group of unfamiliar men along the Camden Road. They gathered about one mile south of Robert Crawford's house. Dressed in elegant knee britches and coats on a clear spring day, while everyone else in the area was dressed in homespun, they stood out. Appointed by both North and South Carolina to survey the area, they were here to settle the boundary dispute between the two states. About one hundred people gathered to watch the process.

The surveyors drove a cedar stake in the ground as they began. The surveying route ran past Andy's home with his uncle James Crawford, which was about three-quarters of a mile off the road among fields and woods. While watching, Andy, his brothers and his cousins might have climbed and hung off trees, picked up sticks, thrown rocks or just run and played while the men worked. The surveyors headed north. They stopped to record their bearings in the form of geographic landmarks such as trees, rivers, creeks, boulders and more, as well as directions. In one day, the men covered four miles. This event was definitely out of the ordinary in the lives of these backcountry settlers. Even at this young age, Andy would have remembered the details of this event.

Every Sunday, Betty, her sons, her sister Jane and her family traveled down Camden Road, crossed Waxhaw Creek and cut through the woods to the meeting house. They may have walked, but most people, men and women, boys and girls, rode horseback. Because there were so many in the household, they may have taken a wagon to church. The area around the meeting house was worn bare by the congregation and their horses. Not far from the church were a springhouse, a schoolhouse and the graveyard where Andy's father was buried.

The original Waxhaw Meeting House was probably a two-door log building covered in unpainted, weather-worn clapboard with no steeple. The windows were open, only covered by shutters or perhaps shades of oilcloth when needed. The floor and ceiling were made of rough plank. The plain doors were made of wide boards nailed together. Rows of uncomfortable wooden benches faced the front, where the reverend preached from the raised clapboard pulpit. A bench rested below the pulpit for the person who called out the psalm lines to be sung. The elders sat on a bench of their own overlooking the congregation.

Waxhaw Meeting House must have been large because some sources say there were sometimes as many as one thousand worshippers. The population of the Waxhaw settlement was six to seven hundred. Because this was rural country as opposed to the city life of a colony town such as Charleston, people would come from great distances to hear services. Of course, the building was not large enough to hold all these people. They often overflowed outside.

Andrew, Hugh and Robert would sit each Sunday with their mother. The Jacksons sat as still as young boys can through the two-hour service, singing hymns along with the other worshippers. If this was to be a Sunday communion, there were also services on Saturday. Reverend William Richardson would invite a visiting minister to preach on Saturday, while Richardson led services on Sunday. To encourage his flock to attend both days, he gave out small lead tokens to attendees on Saturday. Communion was only given to those who had attended Saturday services and held the tokens.

Chapter 5
Murder!

Reverend William Richardson married Reverend Alexander Craighead's sister, Nancy. Reverend Craighead was Sugar Creek's Presbyterian pastor. Nancy Craighead became one of Betty Jackson's good friends. Many in the settlement did not care for her much. She was born in Virginia. Some of the Waxhaw settlers felt she put on airs, meaning her ways were more like those of the wealthy elite rather than their own less prosperous and less refined backgrounds.

Reverend William Richardson and his wife lived in a two-story log house not far from the church. He was in his forties and owned four slaves. Greek, Hebrew and Latin books lined his study shelves next to the classics. Reverend Richardson directed Waxhaw Academy, the school at the Waxhaw Meeting House, which offered Greek and Latin instruction. The literary evenings he held were always anticipated and regarded with awe, in stark contrast to the regular frontier social events of cockfights, log rolling and funerals. People traveled from far away to attend these literary evenings, just as they would travel from far away to attend the reverend's soon-to-be funeral.

Traveling around the community on regular visits, Richardson often stopped at the James Crawford home. Part of his job was to pray for and with the families, as well as to make sure the children were properly educated. This included making sure the parents taught their children the Westminster Catechism of the Presbyterian faith, which defined right and wrong in their minds. Betty Jackson had high hopes for Andy to become a minister someday, which meant an education that included studying the classics. She would have listened closely to what Reverend Richardson, as well as his wife, Nancy, had to say.

One hot July afternoon, Nancy had just returned from a quilting party. She was just putting away her supplies when there was a knock on the door. "Hello! Won't you come in?" Nancy smiled as she brushed a sprig of hair from her sticky forehead. "Reverend Richardson is in his study." This is how Nancy Craighead Richardson may have greeted William Boyd on July 20, 1771. He had traveled from Rocky Creek to the west of the Catawba River to seek the reverend's counsel for a new Irish settlement.

Upon opening the door to the study, Nancy lifted her hand to her mouth as she shrieked and cried uncontrollably. Her husband sat behind his desk with his hand clasped in prayer, dead, with a bridle wrapped around his throat. The circuit lawyers and judges were not local, so the church trustees were notified. They decided to keep the bridle aspect of his death from the parishioners. This made it seem as though he died of natural causes. Evidence, though, suggested either murder or suicide. They knew, though, as did Nancy, that the reverend suffered from depression, though they may not have had a name for it at that time. His long, solitary rides through the countryside had become longer. His silences, which were hard for Nancy to bear, had become deeper. The glass panes that the reverend had purchased for the windows of their home, a sign of prosperity, sat uninstalled.

Soon after her husband's burial, Nancy married Charles Dunlap. Tongues wagged at this quick marriage as news leaked out about the bridle. Neighbors could not help but wonder whether the reverend's death was suicide or murder rather than natural causes. It came to light that two of the church trustees who had decided to hold back news of the bridle were members of the Dunlap family. When this relationship between Nancy's new husband and the church trustees came out, Nancy was publicly accused of murder. People gossiped. What could not be answered, however, was whether she murdered her husband or whether he was murdered by someone else.

The rumors and speculation continued a year after Reverend Richardson's death. Andy was five by this time. With Betty Jackson being a regular churchgoer and Nancy's friend, it is likely that young Andy was present when the townspeople gathered at the church to determine Nancy's innocence or guilt. According to the wisdom of the ancient Scottish clans, they must dig up Richardson's body.

Enter another twist to this mystery: Archibald Davie was Nancy's brother-in-law who had lived off Reverend Richardson's wealth while he was living and would like to have it continue that way after his death. In his eyes, if Nancy was found innocent, he would need to be very concerned about his future in light of her marriage; however, if she was found guilty, he might stand to inherit money from Reverend Richardson's estate.

The day came that the grave was opened and the body exhumed. Imagine Nancy's horror as she was directed to place her finger upon the skull of her deceased husband. She knew that if her finger bled, she was a murderer by clan tradition. Slowly and carefully, she touched the skull. Her finger did not bleed! Archibald Davie shouted in anger, grabbed her fingers and shoved them hard against the skull. He stared in disbelief and regret as Nancy raised her hand in triumph, sobbing hysterically. No blood. According to Scottish tradition, she was innocent. She jerked her hand away and gave her brother-in-law a cold stare. She moved away from her deceased husband's corpse and toward her new husband, family and friends. The cause of Reverend Richardson's death, suicide or murder, was never determined.

Chapter 6
A Wedding and a Wake

When Andy was about seven years old, he attended his cousin Tommy's wedding. Tommy Crawford, the oldest son of James and Jane, was now in his early twenties. His bride, Elizabeth Stephenson, was twenty-one. A backcountry Irish wedding was a cause for considerable celebration. It was not a short event. The day began with Tommy and his family, friends and neighbors riding two by two to the Stephenson home. Along the way, guns were randomly fired in the air as the group hooped and hollered while drinking from a communal whiskey bottle. Andy and his family would have been part of this procession, though not everyone was shooting and drinking. When they arrived at the Stephenson home, they treated the bride's party to a round of whiskey before the wedding began.

Both the bride and groom were dressed in their best clothes. The couple stood before the minister for a sermon on the institution of marriage according to Scripture. As Tommy and Elizabeth held hands, the minister closed with a blessing. Then, the feasting and celebration began.

The Stephensons had long wooden tables set out in the yard with a wide variety of food. There would have been venison, turkey, ham and sausage to choose from with cornbread, wheat bread and a lot of butter. Side dishes included homegrown vegetables and fruits. To drink, they had cold buttermilk, just pulled from the spring, along with whiskey, cider and peach brandy to complete the celebration.

After this huge meal, there was more fun. Off to the side, the men participated in shooting matches and athletic contests or danced jigs with the ladies to fiddle music. They didn't always dance in step with the music. There was nothing wrong with that. They were just there to have a good time while celebrating the marriage of Tommy and Elizabeth. Older members of the wedding party may have sat to the side and told stories. Younger boys would have found a place a bit off from the house to build a fire. They then ran, jumped, wrestled and boxed while older boys refereed. Andy was an energetic participant who honed his reputation for athleticism at events like this, even at this young age. These wedding events, which sometimes resulted in a few fistfights, continued on into the night and for several days thereafter.

Sometime after Tommy's wedding, the exact time is not known, Tommy's mother died. This was Betty's sister Jane and Andy's aunt. The locals would have gathered at the James Crawford home for a standard Irish wake, much as they did at the Jackson home when Betty's husband, Andy's father, died. Betty and her sisters prepared light food for their guests, perhaps bread with ham or turkey. Of course, the whiskey bottle was passed around. Jane's body was placed in the center of the room. Just as with Andy's father, coins were placed on her eyes and a plate of salt on her chest. Everyone gathered to stay up with the body and the family through the night. The goal was to protect the body and keep the family company during this time of grief, so people gathered tight around the Crawford family.

Talk grew to whispers until the night became quiet. Andy and his brothers climbed the ladder to the loft upstairs to go to sleep. James and his sons, Tommy, Jim, Joey and Will, were ready with the others to stay up all night with the body, according to Irish tradition. Some folks went home, some went outside for a bit and others stayed the night.

The next day, Jane was not buried at the church. Since the community was without a minister, a graveside service was probably held on the Crawford homestead, with family and friends gathered around reciting the customary Irish Presbyterian prayers. The sister Betty was closest to was now gone. She took care of the Crawford household on her own now with the help of James and the boys.

Chapter 7
Political Unrest in the Colonies

The Carolina backcountry was rural and isolated. While the Waxhaw settlers read about news happening in other colonies, it did not affect them until the war came to them. What was happening in the other colonies that would lead to war with Britain?

In the eighteenth century, the British Empire spread far and wide in the world to include the American colonies. Britain had not interfered much with these colonies until the French and Indian War, fought from 1756 to 1763, took such a toll on British finances that something had to be done. When King George III took the throne of England in 1763, he decided that because the French and Indian War was fought on American soil, the colonists should pay for it. He started taxing the colonists, but they had developed independent habits that included self-government. Each colony had its own form of government, similar to state government today. In comparison, Britain was like our federal government today in Washington, D.C., which governs all the United States; however, Britain was three thousand miles away and making decisions impacting the colonists. The colonists became angry that these taxation laws were being passed overseas and they had no say whatsoever in the British Parliament making these decisions. They refused to pay what they called taxation without representation.

The Boston Tea Party. George Washington Bicentennial Commission, 1924. National Archives photo no. 148-GW-439. *Wikimedia Commons.*

The first noticeable unrest came with a tax on molasses. Then came the Stamp Act, which required the colonists to pay a tax, or tariff, on every newspaper, business paper or other document they used. Next, the British Parliament created the Townshend Acts to charge taxes on many imported goods, including tea. The colonists became angrier and angrier.

In 1770, colonists protested the taxes in Boston in the Massachusetts colony. The king punished them by sending troops to patrol Boston's streets, which only made them angrier. When these troops fired upon and killed several colonists, this violent event became known as the Boston Massacre. Considered British subjects, the colonists who had been loyal to the king began to shift their loyalty. This shift often divided the colonists. One neighbor may be a King George III supporter while next door were rebels. The British supporters became known as Loyalists or Tories; the rebels were Patriots or Whigs. The Hutchinsons, the Crawfords and the Jacksons were definitely rebels. There were more Patriots than Loyalists now in the colonies. The colonists were fed up with British rule. They wanted the freedom to govern themselves. A wave of unrest and tension drifted through the colonies. The American Revolution was close to beginning.

Drinking tea was part of daily life in the colonies. A colonist might drink as many as fifteen cups per day. Some colonists, like George Washington, switched to coffee rather than pay the tax on tea. In December 1773, when Andy was about six years old, three ships loaded with tea docked in Boston Harbor waiting to be unloaded and for the taxes to be paid. Tea, after all, was now a taxable import, one King George felt was sure to be paid because the colonists loved their tea. He underestimated them.

Under the cover of night, on December 16, Samuel Adams led a group of citizens on board the ships. Some of them dressed as Native Americans as a disguise. In an organized fashion, they threw crates of tea into the water and then escaped. Colonists cheered them when they heard the news of the Boston Tea Party.

King George III locked down Boston Harbor so it could neither receive nor ship out goods. Waxhaw farmers, along with other colonists, quickly sent food and supplies to their Boston neighbors. Additionally, King George called upon British warships to shell areas of Boston. The colonists were furious! Their desire for independence steeped within them like a pot of their beloved freshly brewed tea. The pot was nearly ready to serve, but how far would the colonists go to break away from Britain, and at what cost?

By September 1774, representatives from all the colonies except Georgia met at the First Continental Congress in Philadelphia. They supported Massachusetts. As Britain continued the crackdown on Massachusetts to quench the thirst for rebellion, the colonists were thinking about what their own form of government would be like should they break away from British rule.

British soldiers marched on Lexington, Massachusetts. The first shot of the Revolutionary War took place on April 19, 1775. The Massachusetts militia responded, and fighting took place in both Lexington and nearby Concord. The fight for American independence had officially begun.

News of the war arrived first by newspapers and word of mouth. Nearby Camden carried the *South Carolina Gazette*, a Charleston newspaper. John Gaston, the local justice of the peace, received his copy each week after one of his sons made a weekly trek across the river to Camden. Other residents of the Waxhaws traveled regularly to Camden on business and either read the newspaper then or listened to the latest talk about the war. Travelers along the Camden-Salisbury Road also provided news of the war. Major events we study in history were happening on a daily basis at that time. There was no Internet. There were no cellphones. There was not even electricity. They relied on face-to-face communication and the printed word. News of the Boston Tea Party, other disturbances in Boston, the meeting of the Continental Congress, events in other colonies, state colonial government happenings, the first battles at Lexington and Concord— all of this was news, not history. It was actively happening around them, but those in the Waxhaws were not yet feeling the full effects of the war. They read about it and heard about it, but they were still disconnected. This would not last much longer. War was on the way to this rural, deeply forested community to forever affect the lives of Andy Jackson, the Crawford family and other friends and neighbors. Those in the Carolina backcountry, however, not just in the Waxhaws, would be instrumental in winning this war for American independence.

Chapter 8
Early Education

With the Waxhaw Meeting House without a minister for a few years, the elders led services each Sunday with help from visiting ministers. William Richardson Davie, Reverend Richardson's fifteen-year-old nephew, inherited Richardson's vast library. Davie was in school in Charlotte learning Greek and Latin. The Waxhaw congregation hoped that when he finished his education, he would take his uncle's place as their minister. This was not to be young Davie's destiny. Through war and circumstance, Davie would soon become Andy's unexpected role model, as well as his military ideal.

Between 70 and 80 percent of the Scotch-Irish immigrants could read. As Presbyterians, the parents took an active role in teaching their children to read the Bible. Another reason they wanted their children to learn to read was so they could take care of themselves in business dealings when they grew up. Andy could read by the time he was five.

Andy began school sometime between the ages of six and eight. He and his brothers attended a small school in the woods beyond the McCamie cabin in North Carolina. One of their classmates was Israel Walkup, son of the owner of the Walkup Mill. The two Massey boys, whose family had just moved there from Virginia, were also classmates. The school was in a little cabin with a teacher in his teens or twenties who was paid a small fee. This type of school was common in settlements like Waxhaw. The children learned their letters and the basics of mathematics. Textbooks often consisted of the Bible and other religious books. Their teacher would help the children sound out the words while holding a switch. If the kids misbehaved, he was there to swat them into behaving. By age eight, Andy wrote legibly and neatly. He had a passion for maps. When he was nine or ten, he attended a more advanced school.

Around 1776, Andy began school at Waxhaw Academy, the log schoolhouse beside the Waxhaw Meeting House, for a fee. Betty made sure he attended. This school offered Latin, Greek, reading and math. In order to be closer to the school, Andy moved in with Robert Crawford, who lived only three miles from the school. He attended along with his cousin Will Crawford (Jane and James's son) and possibly a third boy. All three boys lived with Captain Crawford as long as school was in session. Andy's brothers did not attend, possibly due to cost. Betty held hope that Andy would become a minister someday, so she provided him with as much education as she could afford.

These classes were usually taught by the Presbyterian minister. Since Reverend Richardson's death, the Waxhaw area was without a minister. The elders hired a teacher named William Humphries. Schools were few and far between in this rural backcountry. Many boys attended who were not local but who roomed with local families for the opportunity to learn. Some of these boys were nearly grown, but they still wanted to learn. Biographer Hendrik Booraem has the following to say about this group of students:

> *John Adair, a Scottish immigrant from across the river, was eighteen or nineteen; and James White Stephenson, who lived near the meeting house, was twenty. Will Crawford, Billy Smith, and John Douglass were in their middle teens, as was Ulster-born Johnny Brown from across the river. Andy Jackson, true to the pattern that held throughout his youth, was among the youngest but held his own because he looked and acted older than his years. All of them attended because they or their parents envisioned their having careers as educated men in the ministry, medicine, or law.* [5]

A classical education had not been available to them in a long time. They meant to take advantage of it while they could. While no girls attended this particular school, there were instances at similar schools where a few girls were taught alongside the boys.

Living at Robert and Jean Crawford's house, Andy was, for the first time in his life, nearly the oldest child there. The Crawfords' sons were all younger than he was, but their two oldest daughters were close to Andy's age. Sarah was only slightly older than Andy.

Robert Crawford's home, located on the Camden Road, was a frequent stopping place for many different types of travelers, including cattle drovers, professional men and, eventually, Continental army officers. Overnight stays were common in houses along a main road, and travelers always meant news. Hot topics included Congress in Philadelphia, Boston bloodshed, the British fleet and the Declaration of Independence.

While Andy, as a nine- or ten-year-old boy, may not have paid much attention to the talk, he did take notice of the way the travelers dressed and their manners. They were very different from the typical Waxhaw resident. The traveling clothes for some of them were the same as those usually reserved only for Sunday best in Andy's world. Coats with long rows of elegant buttons, knee breeches of colored cloth, ruffled shirts and shoes with shiny silver buckles contrasted sharply with the plain homespun of the everyday wear of the Waxhaw settlers. Most of these travelers smelled better, too. Not that they didn't smell at all because taking a bath or shower with indoor running water like today was nonexistent back then. Their clothes were heavy as well, which meant more sweat. They just generally took more care in their personal appearance. Their manners were more refined than what Andy usually saw every day. These particular travelers were gentlemen.

Others around Andy held high positions in society in the Waxhaw area that garnered respect, but their manners were not as polished. Their positions in society may have been military officers or justices of the peace. They may have dressed in knee breeches and coats on a fairly regular basis beyond Sunday, and they may have had an education above most in the area. The difference was in the way they wore their clothes, in the way they spoke their words and in their mannerisms.

Andy also noticed the change in William Richardson Davie, Reverend Richardson's nephew, who had been away at school studying the classics at the College of New Jersey in Princeton, which would one day become Princeton University. He now lived in Salisbury, North Carolina, just north of Charlotte and the Waxhaws. Davie traveled to see his father, Archibald Davie, a weaver, who lived near the meeting house. He was now tall, well spoken, dressed very well and had gentlemanly manners.

Now that Andy attended the academy at the meeting house, he also noticed the way Schoolmaster Humphries dressed. To go along with his status, he wore buckled shoes, stockings, colored knee breeches, a shirt with a ruffled collar, a dark broadcloth coat and a three-cornered hat. Andy and the other boys wore homespun linen shirts and breeches or possibly buckskin breeches, shoes without buckles and wide-brimmed, floppy, black wool hats. Hats were worn most of the time by men of this day to protect them from the rain and sun since most of their time would have been spent outdoors.

School probably began shortly after dawn to take advantage of the daylight. After dark, the only source of light might come from a fire in the hearth, a burning piece of fat pinewood known as lightwood, a flaming cattail soaked in grease or a lit beeswax or tallow candle. A typical school day for Andy may have meant getting up at daybreak, walking down the dirt road to the meeting house and arriving to sit on the long wooden benches ready to learn. The students would mix their ink for writing, sharpen their quill pens and compose essays and translations on rough brown paper. Humphries would literally whip them to keep an orderly classroom and break up backcountry fights common among these boys. The boys usually fought bare-chested because clothing was much harder to replace than it is now. In their pockets, they usually brought cornbread for lunch.

John Gaston, the local justice of the peace, read the Charleston newspaper brought weekly from Camden. Perhaps when finished, he gave it to Humphries to use in his classroom for the boys to read. Humphries taught here until the school was closed in 1779. Andy was twelve, and Charleston was under siege by the British. Fighting had reached the Carolinas, close enough to impact the settlers in the Waxhaws. Many of the older boys in Andy's class joined the militia units marching to aid Charleston. Humphries went on to teach in Winnsboro, at the Mount Zion Academy, another Presbyterian school, fifty miles away.

James White Stephenson, Tommy Crawford's brother-in-law, was one of the older students in Andy's class. Heavy-set with a forceful personality, he was not more than twenty-three. His parents did not want him to join the military, and the younger students still needed an education. They asked him to take on teaching the younger students in reading, writing and as much of the classics as he knew. Twelve to fifteen students remained in class. In attendance along with Andy were Stephenson's younger brothers, Tommy and Nathaniel, as well as at least one of the Montgomery children from Camp Creek.

Stephenson's school eventually closed as well. Betty sent Andy to Liberty Hall Academy, another Presbyterian school, in Charlotte. She still hoped for a minister in the family. William Richardson Davie began his education at Liberty Hall. Andy continued his education there alongside fifty or sixty other boys until backcountry fighting again interfered. In February 1780, the school closed because the British were getting closer. Andy returned home to his mother at his uncle James's cabin back in the Waxhaws.

Andy was thirteen and had just completed the longest sustained period of formal schooling he would ever have in his lifetime. Though it lasted only two to three years with starts and stops interrupted by war, he developed values, habits and foundational learning that he carried with him the rest of his life. That said, Andy never enjoyed reading for pleasure. He did not enjoy reading the classics, nor did he remember his Latin or Greek. He did learn to read and write and would draw from his biblical education throughout his life. For the rest of his life, his reading would be from the Bible, law books, letters, documents, newspapers and other nonfiction reading applicable to his business or personal daily life.

A confident speaker from an early age, Andy's education brought forcefulness to his speech and improved his talent with words. Rather than preparing him for the ministry as his mother hoped, Andy's continued studies drew him to the law. Debate was a skill Andy practiced as part of general conversation. He once debated one of his uncles about what makes a gentleman, good breeding or education. Andy argued that a gentleman was the result of a good education.

By this time in his life, Andy was an expert horseman, a good shot and a gambler. These were all skills he learned from the older Waxhaw men in his community. James and his son Tommy were both quiet and reliable men. Robert Crawford had a stronger personality and stern presence, in stark contrast to his brother James. He was also an articulate speaker. Will, James's third son, was more like his uncle Robert in character and presence. Will and Andy were not only cousins but good friends as well. Among the Waxhaw Scotch-Irish of this time, the more outgoing men, such as Robert, Will and Andy, were admired for their boldness and skill at conversation.

Andy was tall, thin and athletic with large, blue eyes and sandy to brown hair. He was a mischievous prankster who could be a bit of a bully, especially around other boys. He was known for his temper around boys and men and his good manners around the ladies. When he got mad, he had an affliction known as "water-rush" where he tended to slobber when he spoke. He outgrew this over time, but it never stopped Andy from speaking up.

Chapter 9
Daily Life

At age thirteen, daily life for Andy and his family may have meant that he, Will, Joey and Robert slept in one or two beds in the loft. During the night, their prickly, straw-filled mattresses poked through the thin mattress cover, making for interrupted sleep. Bedbugs bit them. Around dawn, Betty Jackson probably called the boys down to breakfast. There was no light upstairs because there were no windows. Perhaps they lit a candle before they removed the previous day's clothes from the peg on the wall. They wore homespun linen shirts stretching to their thighs tucked into loose trousers or overalls. They wore no undergarments.

As they got dressed, they noticed fresh blood spots on themselves as well as their mattresses from the bedbugs. The Ulster Irish did not bathe frequently. This resulted in other problems such as scabies, a skin disease known as the "big itch." The symptoms began with slight itching with small red welts and lines on the wrists and between fingers. It moved on to warmer parts of the body such as the armpits to cause awful episodes of itching and scratching. Eventually, it spread throughout the entire body. Andy did contract this at least one time in his life. He was probably treated with a traditional folk remedy of boiled pokeweed roots applied as a compress to the spots that itched. Since scabies was passed from person to person, especially if they slept in the same bed, it is likely that others in the family contracted it as well.

Before they clambered down the stairs to breakfast, they put on their shoes. Their shoes were not like what we wear today. These shoes were made by a local cobbler of shapeless leather. The boys stuffed them with moss or deer hair to make them fit tighter and to last longer as their feet grew.

Downstairs, Betty was up early bringing in wooden buckets full of water from the spring. Several iron pots hung on hooks above the fire in the hearth or were settled in the ash below. Cooked in a big iron pot, boiled cornmeal mixed with milk, known as mush, was served. James, Betty and the boys each had a pewter or wooden spoon that they ate with from the kettle or from a single large bowl. Another breakfast option was johnnycakes, a flat cornbread baked in the coals of the hearth, served with fried bacon. Along with this, they drank buttermilk, what they called sweet milk, from a gourd or a wooden or pewter mug.

A wooden table and bench in a cabin kitchen similar to what Andy Jackson may have used during his youth. Mansker's Station, Goodlettsville, Tennessee. *Photo by author.*

After breakfast, James Crawford led the morning prayers, and the family sang a few psalms. This was tradition in the Irish Presbyterian household. They then went about their daily chores.

Betty Jackson milked the cows. She then carried the milk down to the springhouse to chill. This was considered women's work in the Carolina backcountry. Inside the house, she gathered ash from a constantly burning fire to make hominy and soap. Betty did the dishes. If there was blackened and dried food stuck to the pots, a corncob was good for scrubbing. Bones and other discards were carried away from the house to the trash pit.

The garden that provided much of their food needed tending. Betty weeded and hoed the red clay soil around the vegetables and herbs she grew for the family. These included beans and potatoes. Next, she needed to plan and prepare the next meal. In between all these duties, she did the family's laundry by boiling the clothes, though perhaps not every day. Some days she would dye their homespun linen cloth using pokeweed, oak bark, onion peelings or walnut shells, also used for ink.

A likely chore for Andy and the boys was to hoe the cornfields, which might grow two or more feet high, to keep grass from choking out the roots. Another chore might have been to help Betty carry water from the spring for the washing and cooking. The springhouse was surrounded by woods cloaking snakes, chiggers and seed ticks, a daily part of their lives.

Betty came from a line of linen spinners and weavers. As a special surprise, sometimes her family back in Carrickfergus, Ireland, would send parcels of linen fabric. Betty was an expert spinner. There would have been a spinning wheel in their home. It would have been a flax wheel, which is smaller than a wool wheel. The flax spinning wheels are smaller because the flax needs a tighter spin. You need some of your spit to spin flax to keep the fibers together, similar to re-gluing it like the fibers were in the stalk. You can spin wool on a flax wheel, but you cannot spin flax on a wool wheel.

Betty's linen thread hung in bundles around the house along with stricks of flax ready to be spun into thread. This linen thread was later woven into linen cloth referred to as homespun. As a point of reference as to how labor-intensive the handmade process is, a

A spinning wheel. Mansker's Station, Goodlettsville, Tennessee. *Photo by author.*

man's linen shirt takes about three hundred hours from harvesting the plant to making the finished shirt. If they worked an eight-hour day, that would be thirty-seven and a half days. Imagine, thirty-seven and a half days to make one man's homespun linen shirt. That's over one month's time! Betty, however, may not have been the one to weave the thread into cloth. She may have taken the thread to a local weaver to weave it into cloth for them. The weaver would keep some of the cloth as payment. In fact, William R. Davie's father, Archibald Davie, was a Waxhaw weaver who lived not far from the meeting house. Perhaps she took her cloth to him for weaving.

The process of creating linen thread from flax in the field concerned every member of the family. It was a multi-step, year-round process.

1. The flax seed was sown in late March. Once in bloom in the field, the flax plant had pale blue flowers.
2. It was harvested no later than June by pulling it out of the ground by the roots, not by cutting it, so the fiber was not damaged. The

A flax brake. Mansker's Station, Goodlettsville, Tennessee. *Photo by author.*

roots were kept together along with the tops, sometimes with the flowers, all in the same direction, all in the same bundle.

3. By fall and winter, the fiber of the plant needed to be harvested for spinning. As the retting process began, bundles of flax were soaked in water for five to seven days until the outer covering of the stalk was weakened by natural bacteria. "Inside each stalk are several stalks held together like a glue. The bacteria break that down."[6]

4. The boys spread the flax out flat to dry.

5. A handful of flax was then placed across the wooden sawhorse of a flax brake. The handle came down to crush the stalk and reveal the fiber.

6. Following that was the scutching process. Held against a flat board, a wooden-handled blade broke through the outer covering of the flax to expose the grayish-blond fiber inside.

7. Next, the fiber was pulled through a flax comb in one direction over and over again to obtain the best part of it. This was known as the heckling process. The flax comb was made of rows of metal nails placed on a wooden board with the sharp ends up. Heaps of tow, the discarded fuzzy fiber that had fallen to the

Scutching. Mansker's Station, Goodlettsville, Tennessee. *Photo by author.*

Heckling with flax combs. Mansker's Station, Goodlettsville, Tennessee. *Photo by author.*

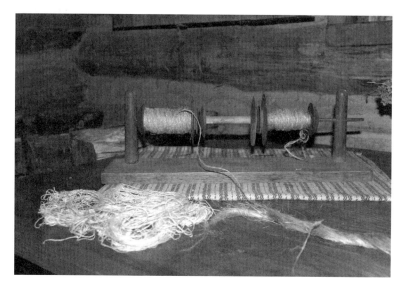

Linen thread. Mansker's Station, Goodlettsville, Tennessee. *Photo by author.*

floor, were later either spun into cheap, lightweight yarn or used as fire starter or wicks for candles.

8. Sections of the fiber were braided or twisted together to form a strick, a holding pattern for storage.

9. Bundles of stricks were hung in the loft or on the walls, as well as in piles or baskets on the floor. If it was stored on the floor, there was a chance that mice might decide it would make a good nest. If that happened, much of it had to be thrown away.

10. Later, the fiber was spun into linen thread.

James owned 110 acres full of trees with scattered fields. The Crawfords grew corn, oats, flax and barley. Utilizing his neighbors' grain and fruit, James brought in additional income from making seasonal whiskey and brandy in a homemade still beside the creek. The still house was located near the spring off a branch of Waxhaw Creek. James Crawford was known for his homemade brew. He charged his neighbors a sixpence per gallon to turn their grain into whiskey. During summer, he may have distilled cider or peach or plum brandy. Irish whiskey made from barley was the focus in midwinter. James, along with help from his sons and nephews, watched the still late into the night. When the brew was finished, it was drained into jugs or square bottles and passed around to both men and women. It was acceptable for the children in the Waxhaws at this time to drink small amounts of the brew, or they sampled it as it dripped from the still.

Andy's favorite place on the Crawford farm was the stable. James had several horses for both riding and working. The stable housed not only the horses but also all of the tack. Tack included saddles, saddlecloths, bridles, etc. Horses were a daily part of life. They plowed, hauled and provided transportation. They were also a status symbol, an impression of the owner, good or bad. Boys began riding as young as ten or eleven years old. Household pets included dogs and cats in the backcountry, but horses provided an even greater fascination.

One of Andy's chores was to take care of the horses. He made sure they grazed in the pasture and were kept healthy. As a teenager, he was already a good rider, able to discuss horses with the men such as how to tell a horse's age by its teeth or determine the horse's physical condition. He knew what type of feed different horses needed, as well as what type of illnesses they might contract and how to heal them. He also knew how to train racehorses. Robert Crawford's horse was considered the finest horse in the Waxhaws. He was "three-quarters Blooded gelding fifteen hands high"[7] and of pedigreed stock. Andy visited Crawford's farm often.

Andy rode his own horse to do errands. His brother Robert or one of his cousins might come along with him. He might take corn for grinding into meal at Walkup's Mill or purchase supplies at Andrew Foster's store just beyond the meeting house. Along the way, he chatted with his neighbors while seated on the horse. Other times, a neighbor might invite him in for a cool drink of water or buttermilk. As he traveled, he might pass a slave or two working in the fields of a farm. Many of these slaves did not speak English since they may have recently arrived in this country, and not by choice. These slaves were not immigrants beginning a new life in a new country with new opportunities. They were forced to become another man's property. At this time, slavery was an accepted part of life in the Waxhaws and throughout the South. As an adult, Andy Jackson owned 150 slaves by the time he became president.

Andy finished his errands and was back home in time for the big afternoon meal. Betty likely served meat, either bacon, smoked ham, beef or wild game, along with sides of beans or greens, potatoes and cornbread. If Andy happened to be at a neighbor's house, he was expected to eat with them.

Sundays in the Waxhaws meant no work and very little visiting. Life centered on worship at the church. The day began with a cold breakfast. When a visiting minister led services, everyone wore their best clothes for morning and afternoon sermons and psalms. Andy fidgeted through church services, but he always noticed the Bible in his mother's lap. It was covered in checkered cloth. As an adult, Andy would cover his own Bible in this same way.

Though Andy attended church with his family, he was known for swearing. This was seen as a defiance of authority. Control was important to him from an early age. With the loss of his father before he was even born, living with relatives and Hugh living in another household, he was surrounded by circumstances

Books were protected by cloth covers and passed to the next generation because they were scarce and valued.

A book covered in checkered cloth similar to the way Betty Jackson and Andy, in later life, covered their Bibles. Andrew Jackson State Park, South Carolina Department of Parks, Recreation & Tourism. *Photo by author.*

beyond his control. All he could control was himself and how he handled himself in different situations. He liked to dominate and be a participant rather than merely observe. He learned to stand up for himself early on in life.

June meant sudden afternoon thundershowers. Dark clouds spit pelting rain, and strikes of lightning lit angry skies. Strong winds swayed leaves and bent trees. Creeks flooded, making them briefly impassable. These thunderstorms did not last long. The sun eventually shone again. People came out of their houses and finished their chores. At the end of the day, toward sunset, they visited their neighbors. Sometimes the men gathered at a neighbor's house for a shooting match or cockfight. Sometimes they would just shoot the breeze, another way to say they sat and talked about nothing in particular. Local brew from a still was usually available. Many got drunk. Others did not. Not surprisingly, some of these people, including an adult Will Crawford, ended up with drinking problems. They could not stop at just one drink. Many of them became aggressive in their drunkenness, while others experienced the same effect more quietly.

Though it is unacceptable in today's world, Andy grew up around cockfighting in the backcountry. This involved training roosters known as gamecocks, trimming their combs and feathers and attaching metal claws. A fight might only last two minutes, but it was bloody. Men would gather round and bet on this blood sport. Significant money was made at the expense of these animals.

In the spring of 1780, Jim Crawford, another of James Crawford's sons and Andy's cousin, married. He married Christina White, a niece by marriage of Robert Crawford. They lived on a piece of the James Crawford farm that Jim's parents had given them. Joey and Will, Andy's remaining cousins in the house, were now in their late teens or early twenties. They soon married as well, moving out of the house and into homes of their own.

One of Andy's fond memories growing up was of the stories his mother told around the fire on cold winter's nights. She talked about their grandfather as a soldier at the siege of Carrickfergus Castle back in Ireland. Nestled on the rock ledge overlooking Belfast Lough, this castle was one of the first and largest Irish castles. It was built

Carrickfergus Castle, Ireland. *Wikimedia Commons, photo by Antiqueportrait.*

in 1180 by John de Courcy, an Anglo Norman invader, with inside walls that are nearly eight feet thick. Betty Jackson also told her sons stories about the oppression of the poor by the wealthy nobility. She instilled in them the fire for freedom and the importance of fighting for what they believed to be right.

Chapter 10
The Revolution Finds the Backcountry

First Battle of Charleston: June 28, 1776

Charleston was an important port harbor that the British needed to control. News reached the Waxhaws that the British planned to attack Charleston. Robert Crawford was elected captain of the Waxhaw militia. He and his troops, along with many others, left to help protect Charleston. Captain Robert Crawford and his men returned home after the battle. Captain Crawford sustained his troops by purchasing flour and pork with his own money. This was not uncommon in the backcountry. Men volunteered their time, money and, most importantly, their lives to the fight. Most of them did not expect pay. Those who could help fund supplies did so.

British Commodore Peter Parker, supported by nine warships, attacked the Patriots at the incomplete palmetto log fort on Sullivan's Island on June 28, 1776. American colonel William Moultrie commanded 435 men at this fort. Francis "Swamp Fox" Marion served under his command as second officer. The British fired three hundred cannons to the Americans' thirty. With so few cannons, Moultrie needed to make every shot count. He ordered his gunners to wait until the gun smoke cleared so they could get a clear shot. Rather than just shooting any which way and hoping for a hit, he asked them to take careful aim before firing. This tactic worked. Commodore Parker's ship, the *Bristol*, was hit, and he was severely wounded. They grounded several ships. One shot took out a powder storeroom on board and blew it up. By sundown, the British fleet had left Charleston Harbor without doing any significant damage, but they would not give up. They would try to take Charleston again in less than four years.

Not long after this first Battle of Charleston, news of the Declaration of Independence arrived in the Waxhaws. The full text of the document was printed in newspapers. America would soon be a nation independent of Britain, a nation free to establish its own government. Since newspapers were a group reading event, people gathered to hear these words read to them:

> *In Congress, July 4, 1776. The Unanimous Declaration of the Thirteen United States of America.*
>
> *When in the Course of human events, it becomes necessary for one people to dissolve the political bands which have connected them with another, and to assume among the powers of the earth, the separate and equal station to which the Laws of Nature and of Nature's God entitle them, a decent respect to the opinions of mankind requires that they should declare the causes which impel them to the separation.*
>
> *We hold these truths to be self-evident, that all men are created equal, that they are endowed by their Creator with certain unalienable Rights, that among these are Life, Liberty and the pursuit of Happiness.—That to secure these rights, Governments are instituted among Men, deriving their just powers from the consent of the governed,—That whenever any Form of Government becomes destructive of these ends, it is the Right of the People to alter or to abolish it, and to institute new Government, laying its foundation on such principles and organizing its powers in such form, as to them shall seem most likely to effect their Safety and Happiness.*[8]

The following men from North Carolina signed the Declaration of Independence: William Hooper, Joseph Hewes and John Penn.

Edward Rutledge, Thomas Heyward Jr., Thomas Lynch Jr. and Arthur Middleton signed representing South Carolina.

While the war raged on in the North, the Carolinas were fairly peaceful for a few years, but news arrived from Ireland about the war as well. Adjacent to Carrickfergus Castle on Belfast Lough, the newly created Continental navy fought under the command of Scotland-born John Paul Jones aboard the *Ranger*. After an hour's battle, the Americans defeated the British warship HMS *Drake* on April 24, 1778. This was the first time a British warship was captured, and it happened on the shore below the castle from Andy's mother's fireside stories. "The inhabitants of Carrickfergus stood on the waterfront and cheered Jones when his ship passed the town castle, demonstrating their support for the American Revolution."[9] In a later sea battle in 1779, Jones would become known to history for the words, "I have not yet begun to fight!"[10]

The Battle of Stono Ferry: June 20, 1779

It was now the spring of 1779. Nearly three years had passed. Travelers along the Camden-Salisbury Road brought news of another possible invasion of Charleston. The number of volunteers and militia in addition to the cavalry held back the British. By June, news arrived that there would be no battle in Charleston as yet. The British were camped on an island off the coast of South Carolina.

Some of the backcountry folk moved farther up into North Carolina. Others in the Waxhaws stayed and sent militia members to provide support in defending their then capital. Captain Robert Crawford led one group of militia to Charleston. Two of James Crawford's sons joined them with a wagon and a hired driver to haul the militia's provisions. They traveled by horseback rather than marching. William Richardson Davie, who had been studying law in North Carolina, was now a lieutenant. He traveled through the Waxhaws in command of a North Carolina cavalry company on its way to defend Charleston. Hugh Jackson, sixteen or seventeen years old, got his mother's permission to join up with Davie. Andy was only twelve and stayed behind.

There was a battle—actually more of a skirmish than a full-fledged battle—at Stono Ferry just outside Charleston on June 20, 1779. The Americans lost the battle, but the British retreated into Georgia—for now. Lieutenant Davie was wounded. Andy's brother Hugh was dying. Word reached them that Hugh was sick. Davie had ordered him to stay back, but Hugh went into battle anyway. After the battle, he collapsed from heat exhaustion and fatigue. He died not long after arriving home to his family in the Waxhaws. This was the first of many darknesses that touched young Andy as a result of this war. They buried Hugh in the church cemetery at the Waxhaw Meeting House. Betty was terribly upset over his death even a year later. Hugh did not die in vain. He fought for a cause in which he believed.

Second Battle of Charleston: April 1–May 12, 1780

British general Henry Clinton and his second in command, Lieutenant General Charles Cornwallis, also known as Lord Cornwallis, sailed from New York on December 26, 1779. With them they carried five warships, six hundred cannons and thirteen thousand men. Their destination—Charleston.

In the meantime, Andy grew tall and lean as he turned thirteen. While he had a temper, he was too light to be a good wrestler. One classmate claimed to be able to throw him three out of four times, but Andy always got back up. That tenacity was a trait Andy would use throughout his life.

News arrived that the British would again invade Charleston. In response, Robert Crawford and other Waxhaw men joined the militia. Betty would not allow Andy or Robert, now sixteen, to join. She did not want to lose another son to this war.

The British attacked on April 1, 1780. For a little over a month, American general Benjamin Lincoln defended Charleston with five thousand men composed of Continentals, militia and townspeople.

A Revolutionary Boy

On May 12, 1780, South Carolina's original capital fell. (Columbia, South Carolina, a more centralized town, was selected as the state's capital in 1786.) Lincoln reluctantly surrendered his sword to Cornwallis on May 12, 1780. This situation would be reversed in a little over a year.

This would become the largest number of prisoners captured at one time during this war. Robert Crawford, now a major, was one of these prisoners. He was released on parole. At this time, parole meant he could return home, but he had to agree not to fight against the British. If he did so, they would kill him on the spot.

Patriot homes were taken over. Some were burned. Property was taken from anyone assumed to be against the king. British general Clinton returned to New York after placing Cornwallis in charge of the Carolina campaign. He instructed him to send British detachments in all directions to demonstrate that it was better to take an oath of allegiance to the Crown than to fight against it. Cornwallis would take South Carolina first before moving into North Carolina.

Since the church school was disbanded, Andy stayed close to the major's camp, trying to be useful. He read the manual of arms, listened and learned.

As battles raged on in the Carolina backcountry and beyond, women helped at home by taking care of the farms. They planted crops to provide food for their families as well as for troops. They also provided pewter household items to melt down for ammunition, hid ammunition and supplies for future battles, provided homespun clothing for troops and tended to the wounded. Anything they could do to help, they did. This was a homefront battle where everyone was touched in some way.

In one backcountry home, Colonel John Thomas was fighting near Charleston. His wife, Jane Black Thomas, stayed behind with their children to keep up their farm. Homes that were recognized as those of Patriot supporters who had refused to take the oath of allegiance to the king were subjected to raids. The Thomas household would become one of these homes. Buried in their backyard were Patriot supplies and ammunition. A small group of Patriot soldiers were assigned to protect the family and the supplies.

They knew the supplies were no longer safe there. The enemy was nearby. Without being seen by the enemy, the Patriot soldiers dug up the supplies, including the ammunition, and took it to a safer location. That left the Thomas family unprotected as 150 Loyalists approached their home. They needed not only to defend themselves but also to buy time for the soldiers to get the supplies away safely. Jane, her three daughters, her young son and her son-in-law, Josiah

Culbertson, got busy. Josiah created rifle slots around the house. Inside, when the time was right, he moved back and forth between the slots as he shot to give the appearance of more people. "Jane and her children formed a bullet brigade, feeding bullets to Josiah at each rifle station."[11] For a while, this fooled the Loyalists into thinking the house was full of soldiers.

When it became evident that the Loyalists were onto their ruse, Jane bravely grabbed a sword and opened the door. She stood in plain view with that sword held high as she dared the Loyalists to come forward. Imagine the looks on their faces at seeing a single woman standing there with a sword threatening them. They realized how she had outsmarted them and left, very surprised. The bravery of the Thomas family and Josiah Culbertson saved the supplies and ammunition the Patriot soldiers had taken away. These supplies and ammunition were later used at the Battle of Hanging Rock. This incident with the Thomas family was not an isolated event in the backcountry. It happened time and time again.

As the British began moving farther into the backcountry, the men from the Waxhaw militia returned home. Once there, Major Crawford, of course, chose to break his parole. He joined up with Colonel Thomas Sumter, a two-hundred-pound, six-foot-tall man who was not afraid of anything. Did the British really think these Patriots would give up so easily? Not a chance. With their return home, they brought rebellion and an inner fire ready to fight against the British. As the homes and lives of the Scotch-Irish were threatened, the Carolinians fought back with determination, perseverance and a style of fighting such as the British had never encountered before.

The war had fully reached the Waxhaws, not just in physical location but in spirit as well. They would not give up easily. These immigrants were here to stay and ready to fight for their freedom and the safety of their families.

Chapter 11
A Waxhaw Battlefield and Its Aftermath

The Battle of the Waxhaws and Buford's Defeat: May 29, 1780

Robert Crawford received word on Sunday evening, May 28, that several hundred British were in pursuit of a Continental unit in retreat toward North Carolina. Crawford was on parole as a prisoner of war from Charleston. He did not know what the British would do if they located him and his men, many also on parole. This made them established enemies of the British. Crawford, his men and several other Whigs went into the woods with their rifles to take refuge. They knew these woods. The British did not. This time, Betty Jackson allowed her sons Andy and Robert to go with Major Crawford. Rumors circulated that the British forced young boys to serve in their army. She would not allow this to happen.

Two days later, Andy and one of his cousins, probably Will Crawford, hid with their rifles under the cover of forested foliage along Camden Road. With keen ears and watchful eyes, they waited. Eventually, they heard the sound of thundering hoof beats kicking up dirt and heading north. A group of green-jacketed British dragoons had defeated the Continental unit they were pursuing. Now, they rode toward the Catawba Nation to enlist their support on the side of the British. The dragoons were commanded by Lieutenant Colonel Banastre Tarleton, a man soon to become synonymous with cruelty in the Carolina backcountry. Later in life, Jackson recalled, "Tarleton passed within a hundred yards of where I [was]…I could have shot him."[12]

The following day, Tarleton and the dragoons rode back south toward Camden to catch up with the rest of their men. The Waxhaw men came out of hiding in the woods. The women had already taken the wagons and were on their way to the battlefield, eleven to twelve miles east of the Salisbury Road, to help the wounded Patriots. Along the way, they met survivors stunned with terror running through the forests. From this battle, Tarleton earned his nickname "Bloody Tarleton." Though Colonel Buford had asked for quarter, meaning he had surrendered, Tarleton chose to ignore the request and to attack him and his men while they were under a flag of truce. Tarleton and his men had no mercy. Unknowingly, he had stoked the inner fire of rebellion to a heated hatred as well as fear.

This is what happened. Colonel Abraham Buford and four hundred Virginians did not arrive in time to help Lincoln at Charleston. They turned and were now heading back toward North Carolina when British lieutenant colonel Banastre Tarleton, age twenty-six, pursued them with a large Loyalist force, catching up with them in the Waxhaws on the plantation of Captain James Walkup. A British bugle sounded the opening charge of this straight-on attack. On horses traveling about twenty-five miles per hour, they charged Buford's troops. Buford had his men hold fire until the British were within ten yards. This was too late. They did not even have bayonets to defend themselves. The British were able to fire three times to the Patriot one. They also charged with bayonets. Horses will not charge into a line of sharp bayonets. If the Patriots had drawn theirs, the British would have been stopped before they could use their swords and more shots could have been fired.

The fight was short. Buford surrendered, and the men put down their weapons. Tarleton's men, however, ignored the surrender and charged them with their bayonets and swords. A total of 131 Patriots died, and over 200 were wounded. Tarleton's men showed no mercy. Fewer than 200 escaped. Buford was one of the men to escape; 53 others were taken prisoner.

Buford had sent his artillery and wagons away, a tragic mistake. The wagons could have been used as a barrier. The four cannons would have been invaluable in this attack. As it stood, the British captured the cannons, two ammunition wagons, fifty-five barrels of powder and twenty-six supply wagons loaded with clothing, weapons, ammunition, flints and camp equipment. Though Buford escaped, he would never again lead troops into battle.

From this battle, Tarleton earned the nickname "Bloody Tarleton," and the Carolina backcountry soldiers gained a new battle cry: "Tarleton's quarter!" These men could not, would not, forget this massacre. More wood was thrown on their burning fire for independence, and the flame for their intense hatred of the British roared in the bellies of these Carolinians.

Betty and the other women brought wagonloads of survivors back to the Waxhaw Meeting House, now a battlefield hospital with a straw-covered floor. Benches were moved. Women from nearby settlements came to help the Waxhaw women tend the wounded. They dressed their wounds with poultices and bandages. They nourished them with food, water or whiskey and care and kind words. Andy and his brother Robert helped. Their cousins Joey, Will and Jim Crawford were in that battle and relayed events of the massacre of Buford's men by Tarleton. This was Andy's first impression of the results of war. This vivid memory stayed with him the rest of his life, fueling the beginnings of a hatred of the British. As an old man, he recalled this hospital scene: "None of the men had less than three or four, and some as many as thirteen gashes on them."[13]

In the meantime, Tarleton returned to the area and camped at Major Robert Crawford's plantation. He wanted every adult male to swear an oath of allegiance to King George III and to put it in writing. James Crawford and others knew to avoid Tarleton. They were not going to take that oath. They headed toward North Carolina, where the militia was waiting to block the British from advancing. James Crawford, along with his son, nephews and other

Waxhaw Whigs, rode through the forest, crossing the road about fifteen miles into North Carolina's Mecklenburg County.

Tarleton was replaced with Lord Francis Rawdon, commander of the Volunteers of Ireland. He was from County Down in Ireland, and many of these immigrants may have known him. The British hoped that Irish-born Rawdon, a tall man of twenty-six, could relate to these Carolina Irish. The plan backfired. Rawdon represented the landlord whom the Irish had worked for as tenant farmers and had escaped from to build new lives in America. To most of them, he represented British oppression. No relationship bridge would be built from that replacement.

A few of the Ulster men who deserted from the American army, however, joined up with Rawdon on his march to the Waxhaws on Saturday, June 10. These were men who took the oath of allegiance to the British Crown. Some of these men took the oath willingly. Others were Whigs at heart and took the oath out of fear or a hope that things would calm down and the war would end. Their headquarters were on Camp Creek at the farm of John Leslie. John was Betty Jackson's brother-in-law, married to her sister Mary. This meant he was Andy's uncle.

Rawdon moved his troops on June 12 to Hanging Rock on the Camden Road near the Waxhaws. He then rode on to Camden. It was now safe for Andy, his uncle, cousins and their neighbors to return to South Carolina. During this summer of 1780, Andy listened to the issues and observed the men around him. He observed the beginning of William R. Davie's career and would later describe him as "the best commander he had ever known."[14]

The men made plans, but the South Carolina government had collapsed. Along with it went the state's financial support of the militia. Major Crawford, George Dunlap and Robert Montgomery would be able to gather two or three hundred men when needed to fight, but that would not be enough to go up against Rawdon or Tarleton. They would need help. If they went into North Carolina to join the militia, that meant leaving their homes and families unprotected. Some men did this. Will Crawford, Andy's cousin and James Crawford's son, may have joined up with one company of North Carolina militia at this time. James and Major

Crawford had large families and quite a bit of land. At this time, they chose to stay put.

On June 14, they received news of a British attack on Irish settlements west of the Catawba River. The attack had occurred on Sunday, June 11. The British captain was a Loyalist from New York or Pennsylvania named Christian Huck. His orders were to arrest Presbyterian ministers William Martin and John Simpson. They, like most Irish Presbyterian ministers, were preaching from the pulpit against the British. Huck and his men captured Martin, but Simpson was preaching at another location that day. Instead, they burned his house to the ground, stole his possessions and raided other nearby homes. One man was shot merely for resisting the theft of a bridle.

The continued targeted attacks on backcountry Presbyterian ministers resounded chorded fear among residents. Men from both sides of the river left to join a militia company in North Carolina. A few days later, British commander Henry Clinton decided that the oath backcountry settlers took not to fight against the British was not enough. Beginning June 20, residents would need to take an oath to fight with the British against their fellow Americans if asked to do so. This crossed a line for them. More men left to join North Carolina militia troops against the British.

James and Robert Crawford and other Waxhaw community leaders like Andrew Foster and George Dunlap began to organize a resistance. Many of their discussions took place in the homes of James and Robert Crawford. All ears, Andy must have listened with keen interest and steady intent.

The hundreds of South Carolina men who initially joined the North Carolina militia now formed their own militia company. On June 15, they selected Thomas Sumter, a militia colonel originally from Virginia who now lived in Camden, as their leader. In May, Tarleton had burned down Sumter's home. The dark-haired Sumter, forty-five, was more than ready for the challenge of leadership against the British.

In late June, Sumter moved his men to a branch of Sugar Creek on the state line. This camp was at the edge of a forested fifteen-mile tract of Catawba land. Sumter called for recruits and received a resounding response. Will Crawford joined Sumter on June 21. Tommy Crawford followed on June 23, with their brother Jim joining them on June 25. Also on the twenty-fifth, George Dunlap, Robert Montgomery and Robert Crawford rode with their entire companies to pledge support to Sumter and eradicate the British from South Carolina. In doing so, these leaders risked hanging because they were either now or continued to be in violation of their paroles. Catawba chief New River also joined forces with Sumter while Andrew Foster, a Waxhaw storekeeper, became Sumter's quartermaster.

With horses saddled and rifles ready, Waxhaw men responded in mass numbers to Sumter's call for recruits. They came whether or not they had taken the oath of allegiance to the British. It was time to unite their forces. To prepare for battle, all these recruits drilled with Sumter's men on Clem's Branch. At night, they returned to their farms. The process began again the next day.

Betty Jackson allowed Andy and Robert to run drills with the soldiers, but she would not allow them to fight. The boys were at Sumter's camp frequently. They helped wherever they could, and they learned as much as they could. They helped unload the supply wagons from the Waxhaw farmers loaded with flour and meat for the soldiers. When Lord Rawdon heard about these supplies, he was furious. When the locals had taken the oath of allegiance to the British Crown, they told him they were poor and there was little grain or meat. Rawdon was upset that the Waxhaw people had played both sides of the fence.

With no state support to fund the militia, Sumter did what he could to train the troops with what he had. There was no extra powder or ammunition for practice shooting, so the training focused on strength training, agility, speed and strategy. They exercised, raced, wrestled and jumped. They had grown up with hunting, so they were already good shots. Waxhaw women contributed pewter dishes and utensils to melt down for bullets. This would not be enough for battle. In fact, they had nothing that a traditional army would have had. They had no medical supplies, cannons, cooking equipment or official uniforms, except for Sumter and a few officers. Most of them wore their everyday work clothes, which consisted of a homespun linen shirt or a hunting shirt with a pair of trousers or

A militia uniform. Andrew Jackson State Park, South Carolina Department of Parks, Recreation & Tourism. *Photo by author.*

overalls and a wool hat. They did have their horses and guns. By the beginning of July, their greatest asset was their numbers. Several hundred or maybe even one thousand of them were now united with Sumter to fight the British.

Around the time Sumter's troops gathered at Sugar Creek, William R. Davie and his cavalry were in the Waxhaws protecting the state borders. Every day there were skirmishes between his troops and the British. The frequency of these encounters decreased as the British realized the possibility of the damage these backcountry Patriots could do.

Davie was now a major in the North Carolina militia. Tall and lean, Davie's dark hair topped a long, thin face with a nose to match. He was a good horseman. While he was methodical and cautious, he was also aggressive. Davie's genteel manners, incisive speech, loud voice and sharp military skills led even a few of Robert Crawford's men to serve under this twenty-four-year-old commander. Davie met with Robert Crawford at Crawford's home to discuss operations and strategy with him. Though they were not close and were eleven years apart, Andy respected and learned from Davie's military skills as well as his uncle's.

Rawdon had not forgotten about the grain. In early July, he sent a unit to the Waxhaws to confiscate the remaining wheat. Davie and Sumter worked together. Their men were ready. At the shallow part of Waxhaw Creek, about a mile from Andy's home, they planned an ambush of Rawdon's men. Davie's troops waited astride their horses while one hundred armed men on foot waited in the woods overlooking the north side of the creek. Five hundred of Sumter's men hid with their rifles ready in the woods west of the road. Rawdon's men would be trapped. Unfortunately, informers leaked information about the ambush awaiting them. Rawdon's men retreated back to Camden while Davie's and Sumter's men waited in vain all night. While they did not see battle, this was a good training session in strategic planning.

Sumter sent his troops home around July 9 or 10 to harvest their wheat. In the meantime, he searched the backcountry for ammunition. Davie's cavalry stayed behind to protect the Waxhaw community.

Chapter 12
Andy First Witnesses Battle

The Battle of Williamson's Plantation (Huck's Defeat): July 12, 1780

After the fall of Charleston to the British, Tories ransacked South Carolina. They destroyed Patriot crops, burned their homes and murdered residents. Captain Christian Huck led a group of these Tories in the backcountry. Huck was despised by the locals. Irish-born William Hill became one of his victims. He owned Hill's Ironworks on Allison's Creek near the Catawba River, just fourteen miles from King's Mountain. There, he and his workers made farm tools, smith's tools, kitchen wares, guns, cannons and ammunition. He happily furnished supplies to the Patriots at Charleston. Huck found out about his allegiance and burned down his ironworks. Additionally, Hill lost his home, grain mill, sawmill and workers' homes. After this happened, he joined up with Sumter's men and fought in many battles, including the Battle of Hanging Rock.

Huck shocked and insulted the backcountry settlers with his profanity in addition to attacking their religion. He burned the library and home of Reverend John Simpson, a Whig leader and influential Presbyterian minister who preached from the pulpit

A Liberty or Death fireback forged at William Hill's Ironworks. *Collection of the Museum of Early Southern Decorative Arts, Old Salem Museums & Gardens.*

against the British. This is just a sample of the horrific destruction caused by Captain Huck and his men. Huck led a group of 115 of these murderous Tories in a backcountry search for Patriot ringleader Colonel William Bratton and his troops. This would prove to be a fatal mistake.

Colonel Bratton used unconventional tactics in his fighting, much like Colonel Francis "Swamp Fox" Marion. He and others in the backcountry led small commands of primarily state militia. With these small bands, they conducted hit-and-run attacks on the British. Patriots kept secret camps throughout the Carolinas to strike when least expected.

On July 11, Huck's Tory militia arrived at Bratton's home in the late afternoon. One of them threatened Bratton's wife, Martha, with a reaping hook if she did not tell him Bratton's location. She would not talk. A Loyalist officer from nearby Camden, who likely knew the family, stepped in to save Martha's life. Local tradition has it that somehow Martha was able to speak to Watt, one of their trusted slaves. She asked him to find her husband and warn him of the enemy presence in their home. He managed to get away unseen.

When Captain Huck arrived, he questioned Martha, but she still would not talk. He forced her to cook supper for himself and his officers. He then moved his troops next door to James Williamson's plantation. His horses needed the oats from the large field on Williamson's property.

Bratton and several groups of militia arrived at Bratton's home before dawn on July 12, 1780. One group of the enemy was camped in a rail-fenced lane running from the main road to Williamson's house. Another group was camped in a field in front of the house. While Captain Huck slept inside, dragoons guarded the outside. Bratton and his men divided into two groups. The plan was to cut off each end of the lane and trap them.

As the sun rose on this hot and humid summer day, Bratton's men attacked a very surprised enemy. Bratton's men used trees and the fence line for cover, while the enemy found them to be obstacles. Just after Captain Huck mounted his horse to rally his troops to fight, a musket ball found his head, killing him instantly. Some men fled into the woods. Others put down their weapons and surrendered. The battle lasted only about ten minutes. This was the first Patriot victory since the British had taken Charleston.

The Battle of Rocky Mount: August 1, 1780

The farms surrounding the British post at Hanging Rock had provided all the food they could to them. The British now received their food and supplies by wagon from Camden. Davie and his men planned to ambush one of these supply wagons. Waxhaw volunteers, probably including a few of the Crawfords, joined them. On the evening of July 20, they traveled by foot under the cover of woods and the dark of night. They came out of the woods on the Camden Road four and a half miles south of the Hanging Rock post. Hiding by the side of the road, they waited. In the afternoon of the next day, they overpowered the supply wagon guards and destroyed the provisions. Taking a few prisoners back with them to the Waxhaws, they were on the offensive.

Colonel Thomas Sumter, Major William R. Davie and their men strategized that they could attack Rocky Mount to the west of the

Catawba River and Hanging Rock to the east at the same time to keep these British posts from reinforcing each other. On Saturday, July 29, they were ready. A dark sky filled with storm clouds hung over the Waxhaws, a clue to the coming storms of battle. Davie's and Sumter's men mounted their horses in the late afternoon. Hundreds of Sumter's men, including the Crawfords, headed through the woods to Rocky Mount, with eighty of Davie's men heading in the opposite direction to Hanging Rock.

Davie's troops attacked a group of North Carolina Tories camped away from the British tents at Hanging Rock. Using homemade swords and preserving their ammunition, they killed many of the enemy without the loss of any of their own men. They took no prisoners. They brought back sixty horses and one hundred muskets and rifles. Along with these needed supplies, they returned two days later with a reputation. The British called them the "Bloody Corps." Davie's men had learned from and remembered Tarleton.

Sumter's attack was not successful, but while there, his scouts observed hundreds of men marching in from Hanging Rock. Sumter was not giving up. In fact, that summer he earned the nickname "the Gamecock." Like a champion fighting cock, he would absorb a blow or a loss and come back fighting. Sumter knew these British reinforcements at Rocky Mount meant Hanging Rock was not secure. If he and Davie joined forces against Hanging Rock, they may win the battle.

Sumter needed to get his men back across the river. The Catawba was high, even to the point of covering Direction Rock. This rock at Land's Ford was their gauge as to whether or not it was safe to cross the river in times of flooding. They were determined to take advantage of this opportunity. Wading deep against a forceful, rapid current, they crossed. Men nearly drowned. A few horses lost their footing and did not survive. Supplies fell off and were swept away. Emerging from the water, a battle in itself, the men rested for a couple of hours on that August 5 before marching back to the Waxhaw settlement on their way to Hanging Rock.

The Battle of Hanging Rock: August 6, 1780

The Jackson boys could not stay out of the Revolution any longer. Andy, age thirteen, and Robert, age sixteen, joined the military. Major Davie gave Andy a pistol and, knowing that he was a good rider, made him a mounted messenger.

The Crawfords convinced Betty Jackson to allow Andy to go with them, but he would not fight. His help was needed in other ways. The Crawfords assured Betty that they would take care of him. Deep down they all knew they could not take care of him fully since there would be a battle, but Betty knew they would take care of her son the best way they could. Robert would be fighting along with them this time. Betty understood that the boys were needed, while Andy and Robert were just beginning to understand fully the results of war.

The Boy of the Waxhaws statue by Anna Hyatt Huntington. Andrew Jackson State Park, South Carolina Department of Parks, Recreation & Tourism. *Photo by author.*

Everyone was cheerful and full of anticipation at the coming battle. A couple of Mecklenburg County militia companies from North Carolina joined them. Andy's old teacher Captain James White Stephenson joined their group, along with his local company.

In the dark of night, Andy and Robert rode south toward Hanging Rock with the Crawfords, Sumter's five hundred men and Davie's North Carolinians. On this warm, damp night, the smell of horses combined with the stench of tobacco and sweat to fill the air. They all knew they were low on ammunition, with only two or three bullets for some. This did not bother them. They were upbeat and easygoing as they marched in the moonlight. They thought of this more as a raid than a battle. They wanted to run the enemy off, kill them as necessary and take any horses, guns and supplies left behind. They would consider that a victory.

Anyone without a gun or ammunition would stay with the horses when the fighting began. A fallen enemy or a runaway would provide additional guns and ammunition. That was the strategy to solve the problem of lack of guns and ammunition throughout this war in the South.

A couple of miles outside the British camp, they stopped sometime after midnight. They waited for a report from the two scouts sent to scope out the enemy's camp. Anyone who traveled the road that night was stopped and held captive until this was over. The British would not have advance warning from travelers.

Relatives, referred to as kinsmen, in the backcountry tended to stay near one another as a support system. Andy and his brother Robert would have stayed near their cousins. One of those cousins, Lieutenant Jim Crawford, probably discussed strategy with his uncle Major Crawford, which the boys may have overheard. They may also have heard discussions and plans for attack discussed by Major Davie. They would have listened and learned and readied themselves for battle.

In a clearing next to the home of the Ingram family, the British camped along the Camden Road. Woods surrounded the clearing on two sides. A bit farther away, Tories camped in the woods. These camps were on a hill above Hanging Rock Creek, a landmark rock outcropping near the creek that was large enough to shelter several men beneath it. The fighting would take place on the hilltop. Using a local guide, Sumter's plan was to circle through the woods and into the ravine at Hanging Rock Creek. From there, they would surprise the British at the foot of the hill. They were running behind schedule due to the time it had taken to cross the flooded Catawba earlier. As a result, they were not able to get into place before dawn as originally planned.

Just before dawn on August 6, they captured two Tories who informed them that the three hundred men they had seen at Rocky Mount were back. They had returned during the night. The enemy, the British soldiers combined with the Tories, now totaled more than one thousand. Fewer than five hundred of the Whigs had guns. What they did not possess in numbers and weaponry, they did possess in gumption and the element of surprise. Sumter met with Davie and their senior officers to quickly form a plan.

Using a local guide, most of Sumter's men, along with the Mecklenburg militia, left the road and turned left to engage the British near the Ingram family home. Davie, Colonel Richard Winn and their troops headed off the road to the right toward the Tory camp.

Sumter's men rode through the wooded ravine at Hanging Rock Creek. The burning smell of campfire smoke wafted through the air. Campfire crackle greeted their ears. They heard the tinkling of bells as the enemy's horses shifted and snorted in the waking hour of the morning. They were close now. At the foot of the hill, they dismounted as quietly as possible.

Andy and Robert rode in with Sumter's men. They, along with the other unarmed boys, men and slaves, stayed behind to take care of the horses. Quietly, the Whigs crossed the creek toward the British camp, splashing as little as possible. As they made their way through the trees and bushes and up the hill, they snapped off green leaves and placed them in their hats. They would be fighting homespun against homespun. In the heat of battle, it would be difficult to distinguish friend from foe, one side from the other, without the leaves. Only Whig officers, even in this summer heat, wore coats in recognition of their rank. Both Sumter and Andy's cousin Jim Crawford wore one.

Ready for battle, they stealthily moved up the hill with powder in their pockets. They carried musket balls in their mouths for quick reloads. Many of them carried loaded muskets with handmade bayonets mounted on top. After crossing the creek, they quietly climbed up the slope to the base of the hill. Twigs crunched beneath their feet. Limbs and leaves swatted their faces as they crept through the brush.

Andy did not participate in the battle this day. He saw very little of the direct conflict, if any. He, Robert and the others stayed with the horses as ordered. From 6:00 a.m. to 10:00 a.m., holding the horses' reins, they listened and watched the woods as the battle raged on. Every now and then, one of the boys would head up the hill to try to see what was happening. All they saw was the smoke and confusion of battle.

As men fell on the battlefield, Whig soldiers ran down the hill with items of plunder that they stashed near their horses. They would quickly relay details about the battle before rushing back up the hill and into the storm. Much of Andy's insight into this battle was through the sounds of war—the crack of muskets, the whistle of ammunition, Native American–style war whoops and the cries of pain. Wounded men stumbled back toward them through the woods. Occasionally, Andy and the others heard and possibly felt the flick of leaves as a musket ball passed close by, landing near them. After about an hour and a half, the gunfire slacked off but picked back up farther away.

A fife and drum sounded, followed by the war whoops again. Men yelled. Horses neighed. The thump of cannons echoed across the field and down the hill. This went on for about another hour. Then there was quiet, just quiet. A few more exchanges of fire sounded before three cheers rang out and were repeated several times. It was not too much longer before survivors showed their faces, many blackened with gunpowder. Loaded with saddles, guns and gear, they led their tired horses down the hill.

This is what happened on the battlefield: Sumter's guide led his men too far to the right. Both Sumter's and Davie's men ended up attacking the same group of Tories. Both sides were low on ammunition. After they used the few shots they had, they used their weapons as clubs. The enemy fought briefly before running away to join the Prince of Wales regiment in the center of camp. Sumter and Davie headed their troops in that direction.

It was now Ireland against Ireland, as the men of both units were primarily Irish-born. This was the heaviest part of the battle. When a traditional British march-forward move was attempted with fife and drum playing and bayonets drawn, American sharpshooters would stop them with fire from behind and high up in the trees. With losses on both sides, the British Prince of Wales regiment finally surrendered to Davie.

This was the quiet time that Andy heard. The British gathered near the Ingram house to form a hollow square to resist attack. Everyone was tired. Rather than attacking, the backcountry soldiers looted the camp of clothing, valuables and guns. Hot and thirsty, they drank British rum. Sumter and Davie tried to get them to finish the battle, but they would have none of it. A small British reinforcement squad arrived, preventing any attack plans that might have happened. As the British watched, the Whigs retreated. The British did not fire. Instead, they gave three cheers for King George. The Whigs answered with three cheers for General Washington. After three hours of battle, they left the battlefield with their wounded and their plunder. Overall, this was a Whig victory.

As a result of such similar "uniforms" on both sides, there were sometimes unusual encounters. During the chaos of battle, Whigs Alex Walker and John McFadden found themselves within a group of men. It was homespun beside homespun.

Walker raised his musket to fire, and a man caught his arm. "Those are on our side!" he shouted. Then he looked at Walker. "What is that green leaf in your hat for?" All at once it occurred to Walker that he and McFadden had run in among a group of armed Tories without knowing it. Realizing who they were, the Tories pointed their guns at Walker. One lunged at him with a bayonet. Walker ran as someone fired. He raced back downhill toward the creek. Nothing was hurting, but he could hear something dripping on the leaves as he ran through them. He assumed it was blood.[15]

When he reached the creek, he knelt beside the water for a drink. In doing so, he realized that he was not hurt. His powder horn had been leaking from a musket ball puncture. That was the noise he kept hearing against the leaves, not his blood leaking from his body. Later, he found that John McFadden had been killed in the confusion.

Whig officers were not exempt from being hit. In taking fire and fighting alongside their men, they energized them by their example. Shot in the thigh, Sumter continued to fight. Colonel Winn took a musket ball that went through one arm; whizzed across his chest, grazing it; and exited clean through his other arm. Colonel William Hill took a shot beneath his shoulder blade. The wound bled so much that the battlefield surgeon warned him to stay behind and not fight anymore. Hill responded, "If I die, I'll die upon Flim Nap!"[16] Kicking his horse's sides with his spurs, he rode back into battle. Flimnap (or Flim Nap) was a champion black Thoroughbred racehorse purchased by Hill just before the war for £300 in Charleston.

Wearing sweat-drenched clothes, James Crawford, sons Tommy and Will and Robert Jackson returned exhausted with faces blackened with gunpowder. With them they carried a severely wounded Jim Crawford. They carried him to the creek. To clean out his musket ball wound, someone pulled a handkerchief through the hole it left behind. Jim was dying. Since he was unable to ride, the family made the decision to leave him beside the creek with his head on a coat for a pillow. Thinking they would never see him alive again, they said their goodbyes. The women would return later to retrieve his body and others from the battlefield.

Andy, Robert and the Crawfords returned home late in the afternoon to relay news of Jim and to tell of the battle. Jim's wife of four months, Christiana, left early the next morning with Betty Jackson, Jim's aunt and Andy's mother, along with other wives, sisters and mothers. They hitched up their wagons to their horses for the sorrowful duty of retrieving their men from the battlefield.

Betty and the other women reached the battlefield around dusk. Jim was alive! The exact circumstances of where and how he was found are sketchy. It is likely that a Tory found him by the creek, wounded him further and stole his coat from beneath his head. Another Irish soldier from County Antrim, the same part of Ireland as the Crawfords, moved him to a nearby cabin. Here, he was found by his wife, Christiana. He was weak, but he was alive. Her husband was alive! Many wives were not able to say that. By the next day, Jim was home and on the road to recovery. The Waxhaw Meeting House again became a hospital full of wounded soldiers.

Davie and his men headed north to Charlotte. Sumter's men went home for a short visit. After their visit home, Sumter's men returned to the camp on Cane Creek. Life on the Waxhaw farms did not stop. It was harvest time. Andy and other boys his age were in the orchards picking peaches and in the fields harvesting grain. The peaches were taken to the still house to make into peach brandy. The grain went to Blair's Mill for grinding into flour. The corn was not yet ready for full harvest, but a few small cobs of corn, known as roasting ears, were picked for roasting over the fire. Talk within the settlement flew about troop movement. Where were they? Were there other battles? What news have you heard?

Andy and the other boys slipped off to Sumter's camp to hear battle talk and to examine the horses and guns taken from the British. From the battle, the Whigs obtained approximately one hundred horses, 250 weapons and other valuables. Will Crawford lost a horse in this battle that Andy would appraise for him in a few years so that Will could be reimbursed for his loss. Andy would become well respected for his knowledge of horses.

On August 12, they received word that General Horatio Gates and three thousand Continental soldiers were riding in from the east toward Camden. There would be a battle, and Sumter and his men were needed to interrupt British supply routes. New recruits joined Sumter as he led his men southward. Rather than go with Sumter and his men to Camden, Andy stayed behind to help with the wounded at the Waxhaw Meeting House.

Chapter 13
Down the Road

The Battle of Camden: August 16, 1780

Major Robert Crawford was now a field commander under Sumter. His nephews Tommy, Joey and Will Crawford rode with him, along with many other men from the Waxhaws. It is likely that Robert Jackson rode with them as well. On August 15, Major Davie and his men passed through the Waxhaw settlement on their way to reinforce Gates.

After the surrender at Charleston, Horatio Gates was sent to take over command of the Continentals and the Patriots in the South. General George Washington wanted Nathanael Greene, but Congress appointed Gates instead. The consequences of their arrogance at overriding this recommendation would later prove disastrous.

Gates took command in North Carolina on July 25, 1780. His troops consisted of two thousand Continentals and three thousand militia, a total of five thousand. Cornwallis was in Charleston. British lieutenant colonel Francis Rawdon was in Camden. Gates decided to attack Camden. On July 27, he began to march south without replenishing his supplies. His officers practically begged him to wait on the much-needed supplies. There was little food. The countryside was depleted. He and his men ate green corn from the fields through which they traveled and plucked peaches from the trees they passed beneath. This combination of food, with nothing else, led to digestive problems. In other words, they suffered from bouts of diarrhea, not pleasant to deal with at home, much less when traveling on horseback to battle.

Gates and his men camped near Camden on August 15. By this time, only three thousand of them were fit for duty. Gates made another mistake. He thought he had seven thousand men ready to fight. Again, he went against the advice of his officers and decided to attack Rawdon. To make matters worse, he wanted to attack at night.

In the meantime, Cornwallis returned to Camden, sending Rawdon to a different British base. Cornwallis then decided to attack Gates on the same night that Gates decided to attack. Not

The state marker for the Battle of Camden. Camden, South Carolina. *Photo by author*.

knowing both sides had the same plan for time of attack, their advance scouts collided in the dark around 2:00 a.m. on August 16, 1780. They fought for a short time before both sides realized they needed to wait for daylight.

The fighting began again at dawn, but when the British hit the Patriots with a bayonet charge, they broke their lines and fled. Gates, sixty yards behind them, was hit by fleeing troops. He turned his horse and fled with his men. He stopped only for food, drink and sleep along the way before reaching Continental headquarters in Hillsborough, two hundred miles from Camden.

With their leader gone, Major General Johann de Kalb took over command. He led them with their own bayonet charge, but Cornwallis threw 2,000 of his men against the remaining 600 Patriots. They did not have a chance. The Patriots surrendered. While the British lost 68 men with 238 wounded, the Patriots lost 900 men with 1,000 captured. Camden became the most crushing Patriot loss of the war. It ended Gates's military career. General George Washington was at last allowed to select his own commander for the South, General Nathanael Greene.

Around midmorning of the next day, men riding hot and heavy galloped up the Camden Road. Others drove their wagons fast as clouds of dust drifted over the sides of the road and behind them. Even Gates was seen as he stopped to change horses, headed for Charlotte on his way to Hillsborough. What was wrong? Lord Cornwallis had defeated Gates just north of Camden.

As the afternoon wore on, soldiers streamed out of the woods and onto the road, exhausted and hungry. Many stopped at the Crawford homes for food and water. Tarleton and his men had pursued them for twenty miles with sabers drawn, killing and taking prisoners along the way. Tory raiders were also after them. Davie and others charged from the rear to keep them away from the Waxhaw settlement.

Sumter's men never reached the battle. At this point, no one knew where they were. On August 17 and 18, the Waxhaw settlers helped feed the hungry and heal the wounded. These soldiers passed through on their way to their homes in Virginia, Maryland and North Carolina.

The Battle of Fishing Creek: August 18, 1780

Sumter retreated back with a captured supply wagon to defend the ▨aws. Sumter was not afraid of anything, which sometimes ▨e took unnecessary risks. Though he knew of the battle ▨, he had captured supplies that he did not want to let ▨t to travel with, he rested his men at Fishing Creek. ▨time, Tarleton searched for them with 350 men— ▨ them. Sumter had no idea that he and his men ▨being watched. His men were exhausted, so he granted them camp liberty. Sumter, too, was exhausted. He needed a nap. Turning over his camp to Major Robert Crawford, Sumter placed a blanket beneath a wagon, took off his hat, coat and boots and settled in for some sleep in the shade.

Tarleton reached them at noon on August 18, 1780, with 160 of his also-tired men. Sumter's men were totally unprepared for this attack. After all, they had been given camp liberty. Some of them were cooking and eating. Others were picking peaches in a nearby orchard. Still others were either swimming or sleeping in the shade. Major Crawford was pouring himself a drink of rum when Tarleton and his men charged. He managed to escape on foot, leaving behind his silver mounted sword. Unfortunately, his nephews Will and Joey were captured here. Waxhaw brothers Billy and Johnny Nisbet were also here. Johnny had been bathing in the creek when the attack happened. He escaped by swimming away naked as a jaybird, as the saying goes. Billy escaped on horseback.

One of Sumter's men shook him awake. In the blur of waking sleep, he saw the flash of swishing sabers. Many of his men fought as best they could. Others ran or swam in a variety of directions. When Sumter realized the full impact of what was happening, he jumped up, cut the halter of the wagon horse and rode bareback while rallying his troops. When he saw another colonel running away, he knew the fight was over. He escaped on horseback toward Charlotte. On the way through the woods, he turned back to look just as his horse went under an oak tree. He should have had his eyes forward because a limb took him down. That good whack on the head left him lying there for a long time, but he recovered. Soon, he found his horse and continued on until he came to Major Davie's camp.

On August 18, late in the afternoon, one or two men rode into the settlement with devastating news. Tarleton had severely attacked Sumter's men as they rested from the heat on the bank of Fishing Creek. Sumter escaped, but many were either dead or taken prisoner. This meant not only that the women, children and elderly of the Waxhaw settlement were worried about their loved ones but also that the Waxhaw settlement was now vulnerable to attack. Their protection was gone.

The British were coming! Betty Jackson had to act fast. They buried what few valuables they had somewhere on the property before leaving. They saddled up their horses and filled the saddlebags with as much food as they would hold. Leaving behind the comfort of home, she and Andy took to the road, heading for her sister Peggy McCamie's cabin. Jim Crawford stayed behind, as he could not travel due to his still fresh battle wounds received at Hanging Rock. Jim and Christiana may have found safety and shelter with Christiana's family, the Whites.

When Betty and Andy arrived at the McCamie cabin, Peggy and George were preparing to leave. They planned to leave with a few valuables and necessities, some horses and Charlotte, their slave. Betty and Andy traveled with them to George's cousin's home north of Charlotte in Mecklenburg County, North Carolina. They all traveled the Salisbury Road along with scores of other Waxhaw refugees.

Wagons, livestock, women, children and the elderly crossed Twelve Mile Creek and Catawba land. The weather continued to be hot and dry. They were thankful for this. If a summer thunderstorm had hit, sending the water crossing into rapid flowing floodwaters, they would not have been able to cross or would have been in danger in trying to do so. At the fork in the dirt road between Charlotte to the left and Salisbury to the right, a militia officer on horseback waited. He asked for news from the travelers of Sumter and British movement. He urged the refugees to take the right fork toward Salisbury, away from a possible attack.

Andy stopped early at another house to stay with the Wilsons, other relatives. Their house was closer to the action. It was, however, still within walking distance of the Smart cabin. He was not far from his mother and would go there to help out.

The exhausted McCamie group arrived at their cousin Mrs. Smart's log home near the end of the day. They hid their horses in the woods out of sight. Their traveling clothes were stained with sweat. Uneasy and exhausted, they entered the cabin. They knew they might need to pack up and leave on a moment's notice.

Inside the cabin, because the men were away fighting, there were only women and children. Mrs. Smart was expecting a child. Her married daughter Susan Smart Alexander had an infant and possibly two younger children there as well.

The British unexpectedly stayed in Camden for three weeks. Cornwallis was worried about his supplies and the toll the Carolina summer heat was taking on his men. With the British stay extended, the refugee stay was also extended.

Widow Margaret Wilson's eleven-year-old son John did not get along well with Andy. He found Andy's swearing to be offensive. Andy was also bossy and aggressive toward him. He tended to be very polite around women, but he tended to dominate other men. That was just part of his personality and character, even at this young age. John Wilson grew up to be a minister who never voted for Andy in any election.

Andy did not bring a gun with him, but he did make a bow and arrow. Using this, he shot birds to put food on the table. Another of his chores was to take Widow Wilson's utensils to the blacksmith shop in Charlotte for repair. Men gathered around the blacksmith's forge as they waited to have their horses shod or to have other work, such as what Andy brought, done. They talked of the British as well as community news. As they would talk, men rode through town on horseback, patrolling with their rifles ready. The British could strike again at any time. They were constantly on alert.

Before these trips to the blacksmith or along the way, Andy would manage to find a spare piece of metal. He asked the smithy to make it into a bayonet or sword or as close as he could get with whatever size piece of metal he had at the time. When he returned home, he used it to work in the garden, all the while wishing out loud that he could use it on the British. The foundation for Andy's military and political future was established during these early Revolutionary War years. More foundational cement was soon to be poured to concretely seal his leadership skills and drive him forward.

At thirteen, Andy adjusted easily to the change in environment. This was an adventure to him. He contributed to the daily farm chores by bringing in the wood, pulling fodder for the cattle or picking beans for their meals. Andy liked beans, which were often served with corn for supper and probably a bit of cornbread too. Andy and Susan would pick pumpkins to break up for the cows to eat. They also prepared flax stalks whose fibers would later be used by his mother to spin linen thread. Andy helped Susan maintain the split-rail fences around the cornfields. At the end of the day, Susan would sometimes let Andy hold her baby.

Spinning in the Colonial Kitchen, engraving. *Wikimedia Commons.*

An expert weaver, Betty Jackson sat at the spinning wheel creating linen thread for later weaving into cloth. Susan recalled later that Betty "could not be idle. She spun flax beautiful…spun us heddle-yard for weaving and the best and finest I ever saw."[17] While spinning, she talked about losing Hugh and her fears of the British.

During the second week of September, the refugees received word that the British were now at the Waxhaw settlement. Robert Crawford's home was now their headquarters. British soldiers had killed their animals, harvested their crops and ransacked their homes. They stayed there for nearly two weeks because Tarleton was sick.

A band of Tories who were shadowing the British robbed and terrorized those settlers who remained in their Waxhaw homes. When they were at James Walkup's plantation, Davie and his men attacked. The Walkup cabin was off the main road and surrounded by cornfields. As the sun rose on September 21, Captain Walkup led the attack through the corn while Davie led another group down the lane toward the house. They surprised the Tories sleeping outside around the cabin. They killed fifteen to twenty of them and wounded about forty others.

Captain Walkup went inside to check on his family and say his goodbyes before leaving again. He, Davie and their men left with only one wounded man, ninety captured horses and 120 weapons. When Tarleton arrived, his troops burned Captain Walkup's home to the ground. This was a small skirmish, but when word reached the refugees, they were again hopeful. In typical Davie fashion, the attack was well planned and successful.

Two days later, the British army left the Waxhaw settlement, marching toward Charlotte. The McCamies, their slave Charlotte, Betty Jackson and Andy headed farther north toward the Guilford settlement. Mrs. Smart, Margaret Wilson, Susan Alexander and all their children stayed behind. Many other refugees headed to Guilford as well. Common thought was that the Continental army was stationed there. They were, however, camped in Hillsborough to the east.

Regardless, it is likely that the McCamie/Jackson group chose Guilford because they had relatives and friends in the area. Betty's good friend Nancy Richardson Dunlap, widow of their deceased minister Reverend Richardson and now wife of George Dunlap, fled the Waxhaws to stay with her sister Rachel Caldwell. Rachel was the wife of the Guilford Presbyterian minister. Additionally, another McCamie cousin lived near the courthouse. Margaret Wilson's brother Robert McCamie was a farmer as well as the justice of the peace there. It is likely that the McCamie/Jackson group stayed with Robert McCamie and his family from September 1780 through January or February 1781.

In the cold hours before dawn on September 26, the refugees, including the McCamie/Jackson group, rode through Charlotte as they headed toward Guilford. Major Davie and his men were there planning to ambush the British as they entered town and then make a run for it. After the refugees passed through town, they passed a wagon train of Continental troops moving arms, ammunition and clothing out of Charlotte and away from possible British capture. Rather than on horseback as the McCamie/Jackson group traveled, some refugees traveled in covered wagons. Other traffic along the Salisbury/Great Wagon Road included Continental soldiers and militiamen galloping on horseback with intelligence about British and Tory movement.

It was so cold that the frost had killed much of the corn. This cold spell was unusual for this time of year. As night fell, families along the way allowed the refugees to stay in their homes overnight. Their journey took them two to three days' time to reach Guilford.

A day's ride brought them to Salisbury, larger than Charlotte at that time. Beyond Salisbury, they probably crossed the Yadkin River by ferry. Not far from there, they left the Great Wagon Road, veering off toward Guilford Courthouse and the main part of town. They traveled thirty miles over a bumpy dirt road full of mud holes.

At the top of a hill stood the frame courthouse with its porch that greeted them. It was thirty-six feet long and twenty-six feet wide. A few log houses surrounded it, including a two-story log jail. Most of these log houses were homes except when court met. Then they became taverns. On these days, thirsty lawyers, clients and spectators stopped in for a drink and possibly a meal. This provided extra income for the homeowners.

Guilford felt like home to the refugees. People here were from Ulster or Pennsylvania. The community had two Presbyterian churches. As in the Waxhaws, the scattered homes of the settlement were encircled by dense woods that were sprinkled with small fields nearby. Worship consisted of reading the scripture, psalm singing and prayer.

Guilford was close to the German settlement of Salem. This meant a different variety of goods was sold than in the Waxhaws. Goods may have included the carved and clay tobacco pipes that the Germans were so fond of, as well as local pottery. A settlement of Quakers was just down the road.

In Guilford, there were foot races, wrestling matches, cockfights and spur-of-the-moment horse races. Back in the Waxhaws, Camden was the closest court, and it was a one-day journey away. Here, court was part of daily life. Men such as Justice of the Peace Robert McCamie were held in high esteem. Their responsibilities included orders issued for debt collection, orphans assigned to apprenticeships, orders for road repairs and other legal duties. Here, Andy observed the rules of law in action, the drama of the courtroom and the power of those involved.

While here, the McCamie/Jackson group helped out with farm chores, which included flax scutching, hog slaughtering, cider making, corn husking and cotton picking. Betty spun her magic, making linen thread. Andy took care of the horses. This group of refugee relatives and friends became part of Robert McCamie's family, who also had several sons older than Andy. Every day there were prayers, whiskey and "breakfasts of ham and corn meal mush and eggs,"[18] as well as talk and singing in the evenings.

Andy's time in Guilford influenced him in many ways, from his introduction to law to the friendships he formed. In late 1780, Andy met John McNairy. John was one of the many sons of farmer Francis McNairy who lived near the courthouse. Five years older than Andy, John would often be away from home riding with the militia and tracking down Tories. He would also have a tremendous influence on Andy's life in a few short years.

While Andy was familiar with generalized, spontaneous horse racing, he had never met anyone with their own horse track until he met Charles Bruce. Bruce was a Scottish farmer who lived near Robert McCamie. Their mutual love and respect for horses developed their friendship.

War news arrived by way of citizens and soldiers who traveled between Charlotte and Hillsborough. Hillsborough was where the Continental army was camped. The refugees constantly asked these travelers for news of their family and friends back in the Waxhaws. News of their loved ones and of war also arrived by letter. Whether the news was received in writing or by word of mouth, it was often difficult to distinguish fact from rumor during this time period.

Chapter 14
John Sevier and the Overmountain Men

B y September 6, 1780, the British had arrived in the Waxhaws. Cornwallis took over Major Robert Crawford's home, though Major Crawford was nowhere to be found. The Waxhaws had been invaded, but thankfully, the residents had evacuated in time. By the end of September, Cornwallis had taken Charlotte and stayed there for two weeks.

The Battle of King's Mountain: October 7, 1780

At this time, the war in the New England colonies was at a stalemate. Hope for a victory in the southern colonies was low. Cornwallis was confident that the South, at least, belonged to the British. There was a chance that the Carolinas, Georgia and what would one day become Tennessee would be lost to the British as a separate colonial territory. While the people of this time did not have electronic communication, they did have word of mouth, letters, newspapers, broadsides and handbills to pass along news of battles, area activity and the fate of loved ones. They sent this news by foot or horseback. Delivery was not immediate, as it can be today, but it was effective. The Jacksons and the Crawfords were informed of what was going on in other parts of the colonies by these methods even as daily life continued.

British major Patrick Ferguson was born in Aberdeen, Scotland. He joined the military at age fifteen and came to America in 1777 in British service. A wound in his right arm from battle left it nearly useless for the rest of his life. Known for his marksmanship, he was also an inventor. He invented the first successful breech-loading rifle that could be fired five to six times before reloading. Ferguson commanded a group of Loyalists known as the American Volunteers. He and his men hated the American rebels. They roamed the backcountry hunting them. They burned and looted their houses and barns, just as Huck had done.

After his victory at Camden, Cornwallis began moving into North Carolina. He ordered Major Patrick Ferguson into the northwestern part of South Carolina. Ferguson recruited several thousand more Loyalists to go after the rebels and their homes.

Beyond the mountains of the western Carolinas were the Scotch-Irish Watauga settlements. The men here were known as the "Overmountain Men" because they lived over the Blue Ridge Mountains in an area that would one day become part of the state of Tennessee. They fought in several battles, earning reputations for their fighting skills that had spread throughout the Carolinas. For their violent actions and threats against their families, the Overmountain Men grew to hate the British, the Loyalists and the Tories.

Ferguson wanted to scare the Overmountain Men into submission. Two of their leaders were Colonel Isaac Shelby and Colonel John Sevier. Samuel Phillips, a cousin of Shelby, was a prisoner of war in the Loyalist camp. Ferguson sent Phillips to deliver a message to Shelby and the Overmountain Men: if they "did not desist from their opposition to the British arms, he would march his army over the mountains, hang their leaders, and lay waste the country with fire and sword."[19]

This message triggered a response that would cost Ferguson his life. Not only were his words like an explosive blaze that threatened their lives and property, but Ferguson had also sent a relative of Shelby's who had been in his camp to deliver the message. Even as a prisoner, Phillips was able to relay Ferguson's location, numbers and general information about supplies, troop morale and health. Shelby took this information forty miles by horseback to Sevier at his home near the Nolichucky River.

Sevier, age thirty-five, had recently married and was in the middle of a large celebratory gathering of family and friends. There was horse racing, barbecue and dancing. With the seriousness of the threat, Shelby and Sevier left the celebration for a three-day planning conference. When Ferguson threatened to destroy their settlements, they forged together to fight him before he crossed the mountains and reached their families. They would ask Colonel William Campbell, Colonel Arthur Campbell and their Virginia troops for help.

Ferguson's message backfired. Usually, the Overmountain Men would not go after strangers in pursuit of freedom. If they were threatened, however, they would fight back. They thought it was better to go after the threat than for it to come to them. Recruiting additional men became difficult. The Tories were aware of the fighting skills of the Overmountain Men and held back rather than join Ferguson. They knew what kind of battle was ahead.

The Overmountain Men gathered on September 25, 1780, at Sycamore Shoals on the Watauga River. They wore long fringed hunting shirts, open down the middle, made of deerskin. From leather belts around their waists hung knives, tomahawks, shot bags, pouches and maybe tin cups. The pants were either homespun or made of skins. Leggings and moccasins protected their legs and feet. These were made of leather sewn together with strips of deerskin. They wore fur hats. Powder horns were worn around their necks. A blanket and a rifle completed their gear. Their rifles were the Kentucky Rifle, also known as the Deckhard Rifle. It had a thirty-inch barrel with a short stock on top from twelve to eighteen inches long. Created by Jacob Dickert of Lancaster, Pennsylvania, it proved effective in battle as well as in hunting. Most of the British used the Brown Bess rifle, which had a shorter firing range and included a bayonet.

This was a large gathering, as women and children arrived to see fathers, sons and brothers off to war. It was fall. The leaves were a blast of gold and red. The crops gathered in the barn. It was also revival time. Reverend Samuel Doak, also Irish, preached in the warm September sun beneath the upstretched arms of a sycamore tree on September 26, 1780. Doak was a tall man with broad shoulders. When he spoke, his followers listened. They bowed their heads in prayer before leaving for battle.

While the men volunteered, did not expect pay and brought their own horses, rifles and knives, some money was needed. They needed to buy powder, shot and food. The horses needed corn and shoes. Colonel Sevier went to see John Adair, who collected money from land sales for Sullivan County. Adair had emigrated from Antrim County, Ireland, with his family in 1772. From the county land sales, he held $12,735 but was unable to get into the North Carolina state treasury to deposit it because the mountains were overrun with British. Sevier explained the situation and asked Adair for the money. He assured him that it would be repaid. Adair is reported to have said, "I have no right to make any such disposition of this money; it belongs to North Carolina. But if the country is overrun by the British, liberty is gone—so let the money go too. Take it."[20] After that, Adair and his son signed up for the coming Ferguson fight.

The Overmountain Men marched twenty miles following the Doe River. That evening, they stopped at what was known as the "Resting Place." Known as *Aqone* by the Cherokee, it was a natural shelter of a large stone outcropping forming a semi-cave. Because it was not large enough for all of them, the men camped in and around it. They left the next morning, Wednesday, September 27, 1780.

The beauty of Roan Mountain lay before them. The base of the mountain displayed the full fall colors of oaks, hickories and maples. Shades of red, green, yellow and orange painted their view. Farther up were the evergreen hardwoods of spruce pine as they traveled over the mountain to their target ahead.

Just as with the Jacksons and the Crawfords, many family members fought side by side. In the Battle of King's Mountain, Colonel Shelby's brothers, Captain Moses Shelby and Major Evan

Shelby Jr., fought. Colonels William and Arthur Campbell were brothers-in-law. Twelve other Campbells from Washington County, Virginia, fought. Colonel Sevier's sons—Joseph, age eighteen, and James, age fifteen—accompanied him into battle, along with two of Sevier's brothers, Valentine and Robert. Sadly, however, some family members fought against each other. Because they were on opposite sides, their same-battle opposition was often discovered mid-battle or in the aftermath of battlefield death. How terrible to know you might have wounded or killed a member of your own family.

The Overmountain Men could ride horses through the woods without hitting tree limbs and falling off. They were crack shots with rifles who, with true pioneer spirit, conquered hardships as they built lives in new territory. Led by Shelby and Sevier, 240 of these Overmountain Men joined 400 Virginians led by Colonel William Campbell and 160 men from North Carolina led by Charles McDowell. They had nearly 1,000 men so far, all focused on defeating one enemy: Ferguson. Not just the British: Ferguson. The Overmountain Men would travel for two weeks and two hundred miles over rugged mountain terrain to reach their target.

The governor gave Colonel James Williams permission to recruit troops in North Carolina. He offered beef, bread and potatoes to new recruits. That's how scarce food was becoming in this area. Additional men joined him from South Carolina. Williams went to find Sumter's men.

Colonel Sumter was at the Continental headquarters in Hillsborough. He placed Colonel William Hill in charge of his men in his absence. Colonel Charles McDowell met them on his way to headquarters. He told them about Ferguson's threat and the gathering of men to stop him. That same day, Colonel William Graham and Colonel Frederick Hambright joined Sumter's men with about sixty of their Lincoln County, North Carolina troops.

Colonel Edward Lacey traveled overnight from Sumter's camp on October 5 to the camp of the Overmountain Men. They were on Alexander's Ford on the Green River near Ferguson's camp in Gilbert Town, North Carolina. Combining their forces, they had approximately 1,840 men, with 910 of these horsemen with rifles.

More were to join along the way. These small groups of troops were now one giant army.

They followed a "Commander of the Day" leadership role where each of the commanding officers rotated who took full command of all troops for the day. It soon became evident that this was not going to work. They needed one leader. That man was Colonel William Campbell. He now commanded over two thousand troops.

Ferguson had no idea what he had unleashed. He did know he needed to be closer to Cornwallis's troops in Charlotte. With that in mind, he headed his men for King's Mountain, a wooded, rocky area of the Blue Ridge Mountains just south of the North Carolina border. The mountain was named for a family named King who lived at its base. King's Mountain was sixty feet high and six hundred yards long, with two springs at the bottom. His approximately nine hundred troops could easily maneuver this space. Ferguson selected the site because it seemed to him that the plateau on top made an excellent defensive position. That choice was to be a mistake.

Ferguson sent some of his Tories home to avoid feeding them. He refused to allow others to join him. This was before he learned of the approach of the Overmountain Men. His troops were now fewer than one thousand.

On Monday, October 2, 1780, Lieutenant Anthony Allaire, part of Ferguson's troops, recorded in his diary, "This night I had nothing but the canopy of heaven to cover me."[21]

Ferguson arrived at King's Mountain in the late afternoon of October 6. The supply wagons formed a semicircle on the plateau. Reports were coming back to him of a giant army of Overmountain Men coming to fight him. Though Ferguson kept trying to contact Cornwallis, his messengers were not getting through.

The Overmountain Men headed toward King's Mountain from Cowpens around 8:00 p.m. There was no moon. They traveled in the dark, and on top of that, it rained. This did not stop them. They wrapped their guns in shirts and blankets to keep them dry so they would fire.

At a crossing in the darkness, they heard the song "Barney-Linn," a guard song signaling the road ahead was clear. They crossed the Broad River at Cherokee Ford. Along the road, a Tory reported that Ferguson was seven miles ahead. The rain stopped and the sun shone as they approached the enemy.

Approximately 100 of Ferguson's men wore the traditional British army uniform: red coats and white breeches. The remaining Tories wore homespun. They knew it would be hard to distinguish themselves from the Patriots in battle, so they pinned cloth or paper to their hats.

After enduring food shortages, sleeping outdoors and rainy weather, the Overmountain Men and the Patriots reached King's Mountain on the afternoon of October 7, 1780. About a mile away from the base of the mountain, they received their final orders before battle: "When you reach your position, dismount, tie your horse, roll coats and blankets and tie them to the saddle...Put fresh prime in your guns, and every man go into battle resolved to fight until he dies."[22] Their plan of attack was to divide into groups, circle the base of the mountain and climb from there. They were very quiet. These were hunting men. They knew how to approach their prey. Shelby's men got within one-quarter of a mile from the plateau before they were spotted. On the opposite side, Campbell was near the top before Ferguson was aware of the attack.

At mid-afternoon, Captain Chesney of Ferguson's men made the rounds. As he was dismounting to report no signs of the rebels, a shot rang out. Drums sounded as Ferguson's silver whistle pierced the air. The battle had begun. The Tories opened fire, but Shelby ordered his men to wait to fire until they were closer. He wanted them to focus on getting into position. Indian war whoops sounded as the rebels charged up the hill. The standing Patriot order was: "See what you shoot and shoot what you see."[23]

A primary flaw in Ferguson's choice of the plateau as a defensive position was the surrounding topography. Trees and rocks provided cover for the rebel attackers, which was a tremendous disadvantage to Ferguson and would seal his fate and that of his troops. He ordered an attack with bayonets, a poor choice against these crack-shot frontiersmen. Their rifles killed so many of them that Ferguson's men were forced to fall back. The rebels had a better chance of hitting their targets by shooting uphill from behind the natural barriers of the land than the British had in shooting from a clearing. The British gunshots did not travel as far, and the rigid lines of bayonet carriers could be picked off as if they were prey on a hunting trip.

As the battle raged on, Ferguson continued to ride back and forth on his white horse signaling his troops while blowing that silver whistle. Campbell roared encouragement to his men: "Shout like hell and fight like devils!"[24] The pops of muskets shattered the air, echoing like thunder. Puffed clouds of gun smoke burned both nostrils and lungs as it gathered over the mountain as if in volcanic eruption. The fierce yells and anguished cries of men hung in the air. Ferguson and his troops did not have a chance against these rugged frontiersmen who fought so differently from the rigid lines of traditional British fighting. Trees and rocks were the hunter's friend, and these rebels used them to full advantage. They provided hiding space as well as tactical timing for attacks from above with muskets, swords and physical strength.

Neighbor fought against neighbor. During the battle, Tom Robertson kept hearing someone call his name. When he peeked from behind the tree where he was hiding to see who it was, a shot pinged the bark just above his head. Robertson returned fire. One of his Tory neighbors fell wounded from his hiding place.

Brother fought against brother. One story goes that a Patriot noticed fatal shots fired from a particular spot on the Tory side. He pinpointed the location: a chestnut tree. More specifically, the shot came through the knothole of the tree. A very smart, industrious and accurate Tory used the knothole much like firing from a fort. The Patriot, also an accurate shot, put a bullet through that knothole. The firing stopped. After the battle, he went back to look behind that tree. He found his Tory brother there on the ground—dead. He had killed his own brother.

Historian Hank Messick records this battlefield story: "Moses Shelby, brother of the colonel, was shot twice, the second wound knocking him out of the fight. Someone helped him down the hill to the little branch and bandaged his thigh. Soon the captain noticed a soldier making a second visit to the branch for water. 'If you come back a third time,' said Shelby, 'I'll shoot you. This is no time to shirk duty.'"[25]

Many other battlefield stories exist. When Charles Bowen's brother Lieutenant Reece Bowen died in battle, Charles went to look for his body. Making his way across the battlefield, firing as he went, he stepped behind a tree to reload. Benjamin Cleveland, a large man weighing about 250 pounds, had lost his horse, Roebuck, in battle and was now on foot. Before battle, the Overmountain Men and the Patriots decided on a safe word in case they were not able to distinguish one another in the middle of battle. When Cleveland came across Bowen in the woods, he demanded the safe word. Bowen's mind was on his fallen brother. He was already in shock and could not think of the word. Slowly, Cleveland raised his rifle. Bowen's reflexes kicked in as he grabbed his tomahawk from his belt and charged at Cleveland. Luckily, Cleveland's gun misfired as Bowen tackled him to the ground. He would have killed him if another soldier had not grabbed him. In the middle of this, Bowen remembered the safe word, "Buford!" Cleveland got up off the ground and hugged the man who had just tried to kill him.

There was a lot of seesaw activity in this battle, especially in Shelby's part of the field. Shelby would push his men forward. The British would push them back. And so it went, back and forth, back and forth. At one point, the Patriots were pushed back to the foot of the hill. At this time, Ferguson sounded his silver whistle to retreat. The target the rebels had been waiting for appeared. Riding his white stallion, Ferguson charged down the northeastern slope. In his left hand he held high a sword made of Spanish steel. Engraved were the Spanish words meaning "Draw me not without reason. Sheathe me not without honor."[26]

The rebels were finally able to fire at the target who had brought them there: Ferguson. A musket ball hit him in the thigh while another one re-shattered his crippled arm. The firing continued, and he was hit many more times. Still waving his sword, he stayed in his saddle until a bullet hit him in the head. When he fell, his horse galloped down the hill, reins flying. Ferguson was still alive but not for long. After the firing stopped, someone propped him against a rock, where he died.

Confusion reigned. White flags came up and then went down as men kept shooting. "Tarleton's quarter!" was heard over the noise of battle. Joseph Sevier, the eighteen-year-old son of John Sevier, was one of the ones who continued to fire. He thought his father was dead and was caught up in the anger of emotional loss. He did not stop firing until his father found him.

Rebel leaders tried to stop the killing. In his shirtsleeves with his collar open, Campbell rode among the men, calling out to them to cease firing. His voice was very hoarse. The Tories raised the flag. Firing continued. The flag went down again, but it was instantly raised. Campbell kept calling out, "For God's sake, cease firing!"[27]

Homespun blended with homespun. Without thinking of his own safety, Shelby rode back and forth between the men trying to stop the killing, too. He bellowed, "If you want quarter, throw down your arms!"[28]

At last, all the men listened. Campbell met British commander DePeyster with the flag. DePeyster must have been a little hesitant when he first saw Campbell. He must have wondered if this shirtsleeved man with the red hair was really a rebel leader. DePeyster, however, presented Campbell the handle of his sword, and Campbell received it.

With the British surrender, about eight hundred men were crowded into one section of the hill. Campbell, as he dripped with sweat, ordered prisoners to sit down. The confusion had ended. After only one hour, the battle was over. Ferguson was defeated. The rebels shouted the official victory cheer three times: "Hurrah for liberty!"

James Collins, who fought under Shelby, would later write, "After the fight was over, the situation of the poor Tories appeared to be really pitiable; the dead lay in heaps on all sides, while the groans of the wounded were heard in every direction. I could not help turning away from the scene before me, with horror, and though exulting in victory, could not refrain from shedding tears."[29]

Ferguson's body was carried to the bottom of the hill and placed beside a spring. The victors went down to view it. James Collins wrote about what he saw: "It appeared that almost fifty rifles must have been leveled at him at the same time. Seven rifle balls had passed through his body, both his arms were broken, and his hat and clothing were literally shot to pieces."[30]

Ferguson's clothing became trophies of war. Someone took his silver whistle. Since Cleveland had lost his horse during the battle, he was given Ferguson's white stallion.

Those with the most severe wounds were placed in tents. Dr. Uzal Johnson, a British surgeon, was the only surviving doctor. He treated the wounded on both sides. Those with minor wounds treated themselves with herbs and roots as best they could. Troops slept on the battlefield. Their exhaustion overcame the groans and cries of the wounded throughout the night to let them sleep.

They woke hungry and ate what little they found. They had work to do before they could move on. They were in no shape to take on Tarleton, so they needed to move fast. They burned the seventeen wagons. Horse litters—hammocks made of blankets stretched between two horses—were made to carry their wounded. Litter poles were made from small saplings, plentiful in the surrounding woods.

Tarleton's threat of arrival loomed over them. By 10:00 a.m., the rebels marched with the prisoners. Colonel Campbell and a few men remained behind to bury the dead. They dug two large pits. Patriot bodies were piled into one, while Tory bodies were piled into the other. There was no time for ceremony. No time to identify the dead. They were at war.

Colonel Sevier sent Joseph Greer to carry news of the victory to Congress in Philadelphia. Greer was twenty years old and over seven feet tall. He had to travel much of the trip on foot, but he did so without complaint. When he arrived at congressional headquarters, the doorkeeper tried to keep him from entering. Greer pushed him aside. This giant man with musket in hand took long, purposeful strides down the aisle to deliver his message. All heads must have turned his way. George Washington is reported to have said, "With soldiers like him, no wonder the frontiersmen won."[31]

Andy Jackson may have heard about the Battle of King's Mountain while doing chores on the Wilsons' farm. This battle became the turning point of the war. Why? Because it shattered British confidence, made them fearful and gave the Patriots time to reorganize. It also boosted Patriot morale and gave them hope and renewed strength to continue fighting. As a result of this battle, for the first time in Andy's life, he heard the name of John Sevier, the future governor of Tennessee. When Andy grew up, these two would later cross paths both personally as well as linked to the future of the state of Tennessee.

Chapter 15
Nearing the End

The Battle of Cowpens: January 17, 1781

Once Nathanael Greene gained command from Horatio Gates, he established a base camp along the Pee Dee River in South Carolina. Greene sent General Daniel Morgan west near the Carolina borders. Cornwallis sent Tarleton to attack Morgan. Cornwallis would move his men behind Morgan's to prevent retreat.

Morgan had about 900 men to Tarleton's 1,200. Morgan set up camp near Cowpens, just five miles below the North Carolina border. On January 17, Morgan's men rose at dawn, ate and got in place for the upcoming battle. The main lines were on a ridge between two brooks. There was little underbrush. Tarleton made his move around eight o'clock in the morning, but Morgan's riflemen were expert marksmen who caused the British lines to give way.

As the British began to retreat, Morgan's men charged with bayonets. The Tories ran in every direction. It was chaos. Tarleton was not able to rein them back in. On another part of the field, more of the enemy broke lines and fled. The Patriots pursued the enemy for twenty miles before being ordered back. This was another victory for the Patriots.

A Revolutionary War flag from the Battle of Cowpens used by the Third Maryland Regiment. *Library of Congress Prints and Photographs Division.*

The British lost 300 men killed or wounded. The Patriots took 525 as prisoners. The Patriots lost 12, with 60 wounded. From this victory, they gained eight hundred guns, one hundred horses, thirty-five wagons and two field pieces. The wagons were destroyed, as they were too difficult to travel with. Morgan knew Cornwallis was near, and they would need to move fast. Morgan headed toward Virginia. Heavy rains slowed them down. Engorged streams and rivers were hard to cross. The Tories caught up to their rear, resulting in defenses at the water crossings. Travel with that many prisoners also slowed them down. Cornwallis nearly caught up with them twice, but high water crossings delayed him, especially at the Yadkin River. At the Dan River, he turned back. Morgan continued on into Virginia with the prisoners.

As news of this victory reached the refugees, they knew it was now safe to return to their homes in the Waxhaws. Though the main British army left Camden in January 1781, there were still one thousand or so troops remaining. Patrols roamed the backcountry, but there was not much to see. Four months of fighting had taken their toll on the land and the people. The British had taken their crops and burned many of their homes. Food was scarce. One woman remembers her family ate cornmeal they swept up from the floor. Things were so bad upon their return that Major Crawford went elsewhere and bought sixty-six bushels of corn for the settlement.

By March, Tory troops continued to roam the backcountry. Captain John Land knew the risk. Area Tories were waiting for a chance when a lone soldier chose to return home for a quick visit with family. They knew he would be relatively defenseless and were ready to strike. Despite risking his life, Captain Land wanted and needed to visit his family, even for this one cold March night. He asked several of his neighbors to serve as bodyguards. Andy, his brother Robert and the Crawfords gladly did their part. Andy would be fourteen in a few days and was now considered "of age" to fight with the men. There were eight men with Captain Land at his cabin. Andy and the others slept inside and around the cabin.

Shortly after midnight, Andy was jerked awake by one of the other men who said there was movement outside. He moved on to awaken the others. Andy sat up. The embers were dying as the fire burned low. Andy looked out the open door at the star-filled sky. Silence filled the air, except for the occasional snap of a twig and the shuffle of feet in the dirt outside and to the right where they didn't belong. He reached for his musket as he woke the British deserter by his side. The two men cautiously and quietly stepped outside. They pulled their muskets back to full cock, ready to fire.

Beside the corncrib, to the right of the porch, were shadows that did not belong. Placing his musket in the fork of an apple tree to catch the recoil of the gun, Andy shouted for identification. There was no answer. Andy fired, and the shadows fired back. Bullets whizzed past him, and one killed the deserter beside him. Andy grabbed his gun and ran for the cabin.

More than a dozen Tories climbed the rail fence surrounding Land's house. Andy slammed the door inside the cabin as he shouted to his brother and the others to get ready for the attack. Andy reloaded his gun. He and the others opened the door and fired. Mrs. Land and the children stayed down while the attack continued. The firelight inside created their silhouettes, making them good targets. Andy's uncle and the man beside Andy were both hit.

They put out the fire in the hearth and shot through the holes between the logs. With bullets in their mouths, they were ready for quick reloads. During the skirmish, two groups of Tories accidentally fired on each other. Shortly thereafter, they heard a cavalry bugle in the woods. It must be reinforcements!

They were very surprised to learn that there were no reinforcements. There was only one lone bugler, Littleton Isbell, a neighbor. He tricked the Tories into thinking there was a Whig charge on the way. It worked. The Tories retreated. The attack was over. Unfortunately, James Crawford, Andy's uncle, died a few weeks later from the wound he received.

This was one of many backcountry skirmishes that took place regularly. Their Tory neighbors had gotten used to having the area to themselves. Armed men banded together on both sides. In the Waxhaws, it was now neighbor against neighbor, Whig against Tory, despite the war. Both sides wanted to protect what they felt was their own. Neighbors were murdered. Even more homes were destroyed. Tories would ransack Whig homes. They scattered the contents of shredded feather beds. They ripped apart and burned books. Some of the Whigs even took Tory cabins apart log by log. This fighting did have some limitations. Women, children and the elderly were left alone.

Tommy and Jim Crawford left home from time to time whenever needed by Sumter. Andy and Robert rode with one of the bands of Whigs to protect their home and the homes of their neighbors. These men were their own unofficial militia. They provided their own supplies, including clothes, food, horses, guns, swords, knives, powder and ammunition. To help them, women gave up what pewter dishes remained, as well as guns to melt down for musket balls.

These bands of Whigs lived in the woods, waiting for the right time to attack the Tories. Sometimes they traveled as far away as thirty miles to escape them after an attack. As an example, seven miles southwest of Charlotte, eleven-year-old Susan Spratt's father had a slaughter pen. Whigs gathered there to gossip as well as conduct business. Susan noticed Andy with others from the Waxhaws hiding from the Tories.

In one instance, Andy and Will Polk, son of Colonel Thomas Polk, were pursued by Tories down a lane with a rail fence border. They pushed their horses as fast as they could. Dirt flew as the hooves caught the ground. It was a horse race with Andy and Will as the winners. This type of encounter was a common incident in the backcountry, perhaps on a daily basis at this time in the war.

While Andy and other Whig Waxhaw men took refuge in the woods, they still had some fun with it. Sympathizers kept them fed. They set up makeshift tables. It was like camping except for the guards stationed around them as lookouts. When they were not after Tories, they laughed and joked around.

As always, Andy learned from those around him. His fellow backcountry men were excellent shots. He learned how to improve the accuracy of every valuable shot he would take by listening and observing. He was already a pretty good shot, but as in most things in life, there is always room for improvement. Andy watched and listened when his fellow Patriots spotted enemy movement to determine what they saw, heard or smelled. How were successful attacks planned and carried out? Again, Andy learned from those around him, from the planning of events taking place now and when he was around troops to the actual carrying out of the plan to analyzing the results through talk later. He also knew the risks of war, as did John Land, who was killed in a British dragoon attack three weeks after visiting his family.

This backcountry fighting was personal. Hatred filled the hearts of those in the backcountry who lost loved ones to this war. Andy had now lost his brother Hugh as well as his uncle James Crawford, who was the only father he had ever known. Other young men held hatred in their hearts for the British and Tories as well. One fifteen-year-old who received news of his brother's death at the hands of a Tory ambush recalled, "I do not believe that I had ever used an oath before that day, but then I tore open my bosom, and swore that I would never rest until I avenged his death."[32]

After the war, many would regret the depth of their hatred and their resulting violent actions during this time. These were not men trained for battle. They did not receive counseling during or after the war about the cruelties and devastation war wreaks on people, property and land. These were everyday men fighting for what they believed in, and sometimes that fighting included vengeful acts of violence.

The Battle of Guilford Courthouse: March 15, 1781

Arriving at Guilford Courthouse in February, Greene and Morgan anticipated an attack. They rested their men, dropped off their prisoners and recruited more men. They sent a request to Colonels Shelby and Sevier of the Overmountain Men. Sevier was dealing with Cherokee Indian attacks, but he sent 130 others. They arrived at Greene's camp around the courthouse on March 6, 1781, along with Colonel William Campbell's 60 recruits from Virginia. Colonel Washington's men joined them. Major General Nathanael Greene was a good commander. Greene would often say, "We fight, get beaten and fight again."[33]

On the day of Andy's fourteenth birthday, March 15, 1781, the Battle of Guilford Courthouse took place. The right and left flanks were almost like separate battles. The riflemen caused heavy British losses. Though he had the advantage, Greene was unwilling to risk any more men. He sounded the order to retreat to save his troops for future battles. Cornwallis gained the battlefield, but his losses were so heavy—over six hundred—that the victory is questionable.

Cornwallis's troops needed medical help, food and other supplies, so they marched toward Wilmington, North Carolina. General Greene followed, hoping to force another conflict at the right time. Cornwallis burned bridges along the way, slowing him down. Greene turned and headed into South Carolina and his former base along the Pee Dee River.

In April, Sumter sent word to the Waxhaws that he needed troops to support General Nathanael Greene to take back Camden from the British. Cornwallis rested his troops in Wilmington. The time was right for a surprise, well-planned attack. A call came for a gathering at the Waxhaw Meeting House on April 10 for a strategy meeting. It was a dark, dreary, rainy afternoon. The Waxhaw Whigs came out of hiding in the woods and gathered on their horses beneath the shelter of the trees surrounding the meeting house. Andy and Robert, along with cousins Tommy and Jim Crawford, were with them. All were armed with knives and guns, now a natural extension of their everyday gear.

Through the light drizzle, approaching them from the other end of the road, they saw what they thought was a group of their own. The men in front, now known to be Tories in ordinary homespun, parted to reveal a group of uniformed British dragoons. They raised their sabers and charged the crowd. There was little time to react, but there is a benefit to being on your own turf. These backcountry men knew these woods better than the British dragoons. Andy, Robert, Tommy and Jim kicked the sides of their horses, urging them forward, toward those familiar woods.

Guiding their horses behind the meeting house, they galloped toward Cane Creek. The rain had caused the waters to rise and flow swiftly. As they crossed, Jim's horse got stuck in the mud. All they could do was look back to see Jim being overpowered by a dragoon. There were too many of them. Andy and the others were unable to help Jim. They rode until they came to a concealed bend in the creek far into the woods. They stopped to listen. No sounds of pursuit were heard. They were out of sight. They cautiously dismounted and continued to listen. Certain they were safe for the moment, they unsaddled the horses and tethered them to nearby limbs.

As darkness closed around them, they heard a loud roar and saw an orange ball of flame in the distance. The meeting house was on fire! They were helpless. The British had the Waxhaw settlement again. All they could do was wait. With the smell of wood smoke in the air, the three of them lay down along the bank of the creek as its gentle gurgle lulled them to sleep. The center of their community, their church, was gone.

Chapter 16
Prisoner of War

Andy, Robert and Tommy woke at dawn. Tommy told the boys to wait while he scouted the area. Tommy did not return. The boys were worried about what might have happened to him. Tommy's house was less than a mile away. Hungry, they would go see if he was there. His wife, Elizabeth, would feed them, and they could plan their next move.

When they arrived, they secured their horses and surveyed the area from the woods. It appeared safe. Smoke from the chimney meant a fire burned in the hearth. There was no indication that there were visitors. They looked this way and that as they ran quietly toward the cabin.

Elizabeth and her children—Jimmy, age six; Jane, age four; and a baby—were there. Andy and Robert gave Elizabeth the news of Jim's capture and that Tommy had never returned from scouting this morning. Likely, he had been captured as well. While they talked, she made them breakfast. Just as they began eating, horse hooves sounded outside. The boys did not have time to hide before a group of British burst through the cabin door, followed closely by a group of Tories.

They ransacked the house looking for valuables. Drawers were pulled out. Furniture was turned over. They broke clay crocks and

A Revolutionary Boy

smashed a mirror. The children cried in the corner as Elizabeth shielded and comforted them.

The officer in charge ordered Andy to clean his boots. Andy refused. He stated that he had rights as a prisoner of war. At this, the officer raised his sword and brought it down on Andy's head. Andy threw up his left hand to deflect the blow. The blade sliced his wrist, cut his fingers to the bone and left a dent in his skull. Bleeding and cringing with pain, he dropped to his knees. Andy carried the resulting scars and the memory of his hatred of the British for the rest of his life.

At some point, Robert received the same treatment, but his head wound was much worse. Not long after this, they burned Tommy's cabin, though Elizabeth and the children were not harmed. Andy and Robert, bleeding through poorly bandaged wounds, were taken as prisoners of war. They marched toward Camden.

Though Andy was wounded, he was ordered to guide the British on horseback to the home of a noted Whig named Thompson. They threatened him with death, so Andy directed them to his house, but he took them through a field where they could be seen from half a mile away. He knew that if Thompson was home, he would be watching. Thompson did see them and quickly escaped on horseback, crossing a swollen creek.

The officer realized that Andy had given Thompson this advantage and made Andy pay for this by marching forty miles to the British military prison at Camden without food or water. If Andy bent down to drink from a stream along the way, the soldiers would rush him on before he had a chance to do so. Before long, Andy and Robert joined over a dozen Whig prisoners, including Tommy Crawford. Most of them were teenagers who, if not for the war, would be apprenticed or in school. They marched a bit farther down the Camden Road, where they spent the night under the stars. It was a long journey for them on foot for forty miles.

Through the middle of town, the Camden Road became Broad Street. The prison at Camden was the district jail with a stockade around it. It sat at the corner of Broad and King Streets. Andy stayed on the second floor with only a little stale bread for food once per day. A British officer noticed how young he was and talked to him. When Andy complained about the lack of food, the officer checked into it. He found that a Tory contractor was shortening the rations in order to get more money.

Andy's coat and shoes were taken from him by another Tory. His wounds had not been taken care of, and he did not know the fate of his brother and cousin. The three had been separated early when the British discovered they were related. It turned out that Robert Jackson had reached Camden sick as a result of his saber cut. A few days after their arrival at Camden, a smallpox outbreak killed one-tenth of those in prison and marked many others, including Robert Jackson. Andy, Robert and Tommy were in jail less than three weeks. While there, Andy saw smallpox at different stages but never an infection from start to finish. Smallpox was the greatest killer in the eighteenth century. Highly contagious, once an outbreak began, there was no way to stop it. The statistics for survival were not good. Only about one in four people survived.

Through the north window of the jail, Andy could see General Nathanael Greene's men camped on Hobkirk's Hill, just beyond the British reach. One evening through this window, Andy saw one of the American soldiers, supposedly a deserter, approach the British lines. The prisoners hoped the British were about to retreat with Greene's men nearby, but their view of the situation was cut short around sunset when a carpenter nailed a plank over their windows. The guard told them that Greene was on British lines without artillery. They intended to make a second Gates out of him and hang all the prisoners.

The Battle of Hobkirk's Hill: April 25, 1781

With the razor blade they were given to divide their food, Andy proceeded to cut a pine knot out of the plank. By daybreak, with the aid of a fellow prisoner, Andy had made a hole about one and a half inches wide, giving a full view of General Greene's camp. On the morning of April 25, 1781, Andy had his eye to the peephole

and was giving updates to the other prisoners. The British troops advanced using the cover of the woods in the hope of surprising the American troops, but at the foot of Hobkirk's Hill, they were halted by heavy fire from the Americans.

The British thought Greene was out of artillery and advanced without fear. The British as well as the prisoners were surprised to find out this was not the case. The prisoners cheered as Andy relayed the events that followed. The British were confused, with many wounded and many running in every direction. It was like watching live-action television through that peephole. The prisoners followed any nudge of Patriot gain on the battlefield with the hope of victory. Their joy was short-lived, as the British recovered their lines and forced the Americans to retreat.

Not long after this, Lord Rawdon, the British commander at the Camden jail, received a caller, a spunky, blue-eyed Irishwoman by the name of Betty Jackson. She rode by horseback from the Waxhaws to reinforce the request of an American militia captain for a prisoner exchange, including her two sons. The Jackson brothers and three others were released in exchange for British prisoners from the Americans.

Chapter 17
All Alone in the World

On their way home, Robert was so weak from smallpox and his infected wounds that he had to be held on his horse. Rain drenched them on their journey home. While Mrs. Jackson rode another pony, Andy walked in the rain without his coat and barefoot since both his coat and shoes had been taken while he was a prisoner. When they arrived home, Robert was put to bed with a raging fever. He was dead within two days.

With an eight- to twelve-day incubation period, Andy realized the fever and nausea he felt on the journey home came from his time in the disease-filled jail. He now had smallpox. Andy became delirious with fever. Elizabeth fought for several weeks to save her one remaining son.

Andy fought smallpox the first three weeks of May in isolation except for his mother and the occasional visit from a doctor. During this time, Betty had to feed them on her own. No one would come near them because of the smallpox. It was a very contagious disease. Somehow, she managed to provide for them. She was always very resourceful and very strong.

Throughout his fever, Betty kept Andy up to date on the news. She told him that Greene's troops, whom he had so desperately tried to view through the knothole in jail, were successful. Another victory! The British had evacuated Camden, but they burned down the jail in the process.

Other symptoms of smallpox to come included splitting headache, chills and backache. Andy might have had a few nights of delirium, nightmares or convulsions. Most people survived the fever to see themselves break out in a rash of flat, reddish spots. They first appeared on the face and then over the rest of the body. Finally, they appeared on the inside of the mouth and throat, causing hoarseness. The thickest sores were on the face; these went from pimples to blisters to open sores filled with puss. Andy's skin felt like it was on fire. The disease spread inside to his organs in the same way it attacked his skin. After a week, things settled down, and scabs developed.

By the end of May, Andy's scabs were gone. Some say that Andy carried pockmarks on his face for the rest of his life—more scars resulting from the war. On the positive side, Andy was now immune to smallpox. On the downside, his weakened immune system, tired from fighting smallpox, could not fight off malaria. At this time in history, no one knew malaria came from mosquitoes. They did know new cases of malaria usually decreased with cold weather. This disease could last for months and left its victim, Andy, again fighting chills, fever and weakness. He recovered, but it took a while to feel like himself again. In the meantime, Betty knew they needed help. They moved in with Major Robert Crawford and his family.

Spring brought the promise of food to the recovering Waxhaws. Crops sprouted. Stalks of wheat and corn, though still green and not yet ready for harvest, meant hope. Cornwallis was now in Yorktown, and most of the war had left the Carolinas except for the British hold on Charleston. Will and Joey Crawford, James Crawford's sons, were in Charleston on one of the British prison ships with "ship fever," which consisted of outbreaks of smallpox, yellow fever and possibly typhus. Lice on the prisoners and their clothing contributed to disease.

News of a prisoner exchange in Charleston arrived. This meant many of the Waxhaw boys on the disease-filled prison ships would be released. Betty knew that Joey and Will Crawford could be among them.

As soon as Andy was out of danger, Betty, her friend Nancy Craighead Dunlap and a lady named Boyd set out for Charleston to nurse Will and Joey back to health. They all knew the risks involved. Betty understood that if she did not return, Andy would be alone. All of his immediate family would be gone. Major Crawford and his family were not bound to help Andy should anything happen to her, but she hoped they would. Before Betty left with the other women for the three- to four-day journey on horseback, she talked to Andy. Knowing these could be her last words to her son, she chose them carefully: "Make friends by being honest, keep them by being steadfast. Andy, never tell a lie or take what is not yours. Never sue for slander. Settle them cases yourself."[34]

Messengers, soldiers and supply wagons headed south along the Salisbury-Camden Road. Andy witnessed this daily activity while living in Major Crawford's home beside this road. Major Crawford was no longer an officer under Sumter's command. Whig travelers, however, knew they were welcome to stay at his home. In the area, there continued to be light encounters with local Tories, considered part of daily life at this point.

A few weeks later, around the beginning of July, the Charleston prisoners returned home. Will Crawford was with them, but his brother Joey had died a few months earlier, not long after being taken prisoner. It is today believed that he had typhus.

On the way home from Charleston in late June 1781, Betty contracted ship fever and died. Realizing how ill she was, she and others traveling with her stopped at the home of a former Waxhaw carpenter named Barton. After her death, he generously made a coffin for her. She is buried in an unknown location in the area. Today, a memorial to her rests in the Waxhaw church cemetery where her husband is buried. Andy was given a bundle of her belongings from the journey.

Chapter 18
Crawford's Public Station

Major Crawford was a good businessman. In August 1781, his farm became a public station, a warehouse for Nathanael Greene's army to store food and supplies. Major Davie, who was now Greene's quartermaster, approved of this. Camden merchant and militia captain John Galbraith ran the station. Leasing two slaves from the major, he cut down trees and constructed log outbuildings to accommodate the army's needs. Will Crawford came on to work in the commissary, the main building where food and supplies were issued to the troops. He earned forty silver dollars each month for his work there. It is likely that Jackson also worked for Galbraith, probably as a clerk or something similar.

In and out of Crawford's yard rolled wagons filled with army goods, including food for both horses and men, as well as weapons and ammunition. Captain Galbraith was responsible for checking the wagons in and issuing paperwork to the farmers for payback by the state when the war was over. Waxhaw men who were not currently fighting hung out at the station. They lounged, joked and drank. Some were given jobs driving wagons or guarding the storehouses. Nathan Barr worked there. He had suffered through smallpox in the Camden jail. George McWhorter was a guard and also one of Andy's old classmates. These men and others made time to talk to Andy. They knew he had now lost his entire family. Will, however, was the person to whom he was closest. He was more like a brother to Andy than a cousin. Sally, Major Crawford's daughter who was just three years older than Andy, treated him like a brother as well.

Two units of North Carolina militia left Camden without orders from their commander. They were tired of fighting, restless and found ways to be a nuisance while camped there. Without asking, they took down the rail fences that Captain Galbraith had put up to keep in the cattle. They probably needed firewood and chose this as an easy solution. Captain Galbraith was not amused. His cattle, which he kept as part of army supplies, were now roaming free and had to be rounded up in temporary pens while the fences were rebuilt. The North Carolinians then complained about the lack of provisions. Their commander, a Frenchman named Colonel Malmady, found them, gave them a verbal slashing about leaving Camden and ordered their return. He also arrested one of their leaders. The North Carolinians had had enough fighting, enough orders, enough killing. They ignored the Frenchman and headed north toward their home state.

Tommy Crawford's male family members and neighbors gathered to help him rebuild his cabin, which had been burned to the ground during the war. With his axe, Andy was preparing a fallen tree for use as a log in the house. It was time-consuming manual labor requiring a lot of sweat. In frustration at one point, Andy "threw down his axe and swore that he was never made to hew logs."[35] While Andy did not want to be a minister as his mother had hoped, he did want to do something that was not manual labor.

End of the War

News of peace talks arrived none too soon for the exhausted backcountry men. Cornwallis surrendered on October 19, 1781, in Yorktown, Virginia, one year and twelve days after the Battle of King's Mountain. He did not surrender his sword to George Washington, though. Washington thought it fitting that since General Lincoln had surrendered his sword to Cornwallis at Charleston, Cornwallis should now surrender his sword to Lincoln. And so he did.

After Cornwallis surrendered, Washington sent a rider to Philadelphia to inform Congress. Shortly thereafter, the people of Philadelphia were notified by the German town crier as he strolled the streets ringing his hand bell. With his lantern lit to cut the early morning darkness, he shouted, "Three o'clock and Cornwallis is taken!"

Negotiations for a treaty began. It took a little over a year for a preliminary treaty to be signed in Paris. In the meantime, minor skirmishes continued in the backcountry. The final treaty was signed on September 3, 1783, eight years after the first shot was fired in Lexington.

Peace talk did not mean an end to business at the Crawfords' Public Station. Soldiers continued up and down the Salisbury-Camden Road. Though the war was over, the British did not leave Charleston until 1783. Between 1781 and 1782, several people evacuated Charleston to escape the British, much like when Andy and his mother left the Waxhaws. These people were merchants and professionals with wealth, refined manners and elegant speech. Several of them came to the Waxhaws, and a few stayed with Major Crawford. Isaac Donnon arrived in the area near the beginning of the war with his mother from the Lowcountry, a term used to refer to South Carolina's coast. He had served in the militia, and he and Andy became friends. Isaac frequently visited Major Crawford's home, and eventually, he married Sally Crawford, Major Crawford's daughter.

At some point in 1782, Major Crawford traveled with Andy to Charleston on business. He was to collect appraised damages to his property by the public station. On the four-day journey, they stayed at Gum Swamp at the home of Captain William Nettles. It is likely they stayed with others the major knew along the way. As they got closer to Charleston, the landscape changed from dense woods to Spanish moss, palmettos, sand and insects. They were in the swampy marsh of the Lowcountry.

This was Andy's first visit to a large city. As they rode into Charleston, he heard the hawking of street vendors. In the distance of the harbor, he saw the tall masts of ships greeting him. The smell of the ocean wafted in over the smell of magnolias and jasmine. These pleasant scents, however, could not mask the smell of the beef market in the center of town or dead animals in the streets. This was a very new and exciting experience for him, one he would seek again on his own in less than two years.

Andy's time living with Major Crawford would soon end. Andy argued with Captain Galbraith but, in later years, could not remember what the argument was about. Captain Galbraith threatened to punish him "for some reason, I forget now what."[36] Though only fifteen by this time, Andy was hardened by death, disease and violence, all of which forced him to grow up quickly. According to Andy, his response to Galbraith was "that I had arrived at the age to know my rights, and although weak and feeble from disease, I had courage to defend them, and if he attempted anything of that kind I would most assuredly Send him to the other world."[37]

Despite his rank, Galbraith was not a fighter. Tall, pale, thin Andy scared him. Galbraith complained to Major Crawford. Worried about losing his prosperous business, he had a talk with Andy. Andy would live with Major Crawford's wife's uncle, Joseph White, who lived a little farther down Waxhaw Creek. He would apprentice with his son George White in saddlery. Everyone around Andy knew of his love of horses. They all felt this would be a good way for him to earn a living.

Chapter 19
Career Decisions

J oseph and Elizabeth White lived on a five-hundred-acre forested farm. All four of Joseph's sons lived with their parents. Henry was the eldest. George and Joey were in their early twenties, and Hugh was nineteen. George and Joey had served under Major Crawford during the war and learned the art and trade of saddlery. They were teaching it to Hugh, their youngest brother, and George would teach Andy as well. Andy worked to earn his keep. The Whites were considered honest, hardworking, intelligent people.

The saddlery shop was in a log outbuilding on the farm. Part of the work included finding the wood to make a saddletree. Pieces of wood had to be joined together that would fit a particular horse's back. A pot of flour glue bubbled over the heat of the fire. Andy learned to measure and cut leather and rawhide to fit over the saddletree, which was the frame of the saddle. Various tools were used: equipment for stretching leather, a variety of knives for trimming the leather, awls for making holds, a hammer, different types of vices, nails and needles for stitching. One of the first tasks Andy learned was to set the awl in the leather to make a good stitch. He learned how to make girths, bridles, harnesses and other equipment for the horses. Later in life, Andy said of his experience here, "I think I would have made a pretty good saddler."[38]

Much like a blacksmith shop, a saddlery shop was a magnet for men to talk. Andy wore an apron as he sat at a workbench cutting leather. He and the Whites talked horses, among other topics. Andy developed a good relationship with them, especially with Hugh, who was closest to his age. Hugh liked to read and use big words. Andy preferred to ride horses rather than read, and his words were simple but effective.

If it was a pretty day, they might close up shop early and go fishing or race horses. Raccoon, or coon, hunting was a popular nighttime activity. The Whites' saddlery shop and farm provided a pleasant, lazy environment where Andy still learned a trade. He was here about six months.

During the summer of 1782, Major Crawford discovered that Galbraith had manipulated the finances of the station. He had somehow shifted that debt onto Will Crawford before leaving his post at the station. By October, to escape debtors in the Waxhaws, Major Crawford arranged for Will to study in Salisbury, North Carolina, in the law office of a friend of William R. Davie. This provided Will with the opportunity to learn a profession, a way to earn a living. The public station closed around this time, so Will's help was no longer needed there.

By age sixteen, Andy was once again living with Major Crawford. The station was now closed, and Will was in Salisbury studying law. History is a bit sketchy around this time as to whether Andy turned up at several different schools or, what is more likely the case, participated in horse racing, cockfighting and gambling around the region.

Either this year or early the next year, Andy's grandfather, Hugh Jackson, a weaver, passed away in Ireland. Andy traveled to Charleston to claim his inheritance of £300 or £400 of silver. This money, along with his two hundred acres at Twelve Mile Creek,

Opposite, top: Horse equipment stored in a log outbuilding. Historic Brattonsville. McConnells, South Carolina. *Photo by author.*

Opposite, bottom: A saddletree and saddlery tools representative of the Revolutionary War period provided by Terry Palmer. *Photo by author.*

would be a solid beginning to his life. Half of the money would put him through college. Andy, however, decided not to head back to the Waxhaws. Instead, he chose to remain in Charleston.

The difference in dress, character and manners of these Charlestonians made quite an impression on Andy. He admired and respected them. He sought to be like them. Disputes were settled by them with formal challenges to duel using pistols rather than the bare-fisted fighting of the backcountry. From Charlestonians, Andy also learned about imported wines rather than homemade whiskey, fine fabrics and tailoring rather than homespun and how to respond using the appropriate social graces. The friends Andy made here, however, were not permanent friendships.

At McCrady's Tavern and the paddock at New Market, he talked horses with the men. From horses lost during the war to horses found, the stories were many. Horse races were also very popular—so popular, in fact, that on horse racing days, the courts closed, schools let out and merchants put up their shutters in order to attend. Unfortunately, Andy did not manage his inheritance well. He was broke, and he owed his landlord money.

While he tried to figure out how to pay it off, he walked into a tavern for a game of Rattle and Snap, a dice game. Offered £200 against his horse by another player, Andy took a chance. He had to do something. With a roll of the dice, he won enough money to pay off his landlord and head home to the Waxhaws.

Andy decided to obtain the education of a minister but not to choose that as his profession. He so enjoyed attention. He had seen courtroom drama firsthand during his time in Guilford. He decided he could be a performer as well. Practicing for this role his entire life, he would do as Davie did and become a lawyer. Davie embodied success to Andy. Davie had left the Waxhaws and become a lawyer. He served well during the war, rising to the rank of colonel. He married and had a fine home. Davie, however, had advantages that Andy did not. He had a substantial inheritance to sustain him while he established his own career and to pay for his college education at the elite Princeton University.

Will Crawford also provided Andy with a role model. He was from the Waxhaws with the same background as Andy. He had to sustain himself on his own. He studied law for about two years, obtaining his law license in the spring of 1784. He became a circuit lawyer out of Salisbury. As such, he came to Charlotte every three months for county court. Many people from the Waxhaws came there on business as well, including Major Crawford. Andy would have traveled with Major Crawford to Charlotte and seen Will there in his official capacity as a lawyer.

Andy was a talker. He would have asked questions to find out how to become a lawyer, too. There were no age or education requirements. He did need to pass an oral exam that was given by judges on the procedures and terminology of law. This meant a lot of study time to prepare himself. Most judges agreed that it took at least one year of study and up to three years in order to pass the test. He needed to study under a lawyer with a basic set of law books that included legal terms in Latin and French. That lawyer might charge him a fee to study with him. He would explain the more difficult sections of law and allow Andy to practice writing legal documents in the correct format. His other option was to just study on his own. Andy talked to Major Crawford and other men around him to decide what to do.

Andy chose Bethel Academy, a small school that was only about a year old. The log school was beyond Catawba land, northwest of the Waxhaw settlement and on the other side of the Catawba River. About four miles away from Bethel Meeting House, it was under the direction of the minister Francis Cummins. Cummins was one of the visiting Waxhaw ministers and was well known in the area. Robert McCulloch, a heavy-set minister from Mecklenburg County, was the Bethel Academy teacher.

Bethel Academy was in a valley downhill from the home of Mrs. Isabella Howe, also from the Waxhaws and a Dunlap before marriage. Perhaps she was a relative of George Dunlap, the husband of Andy's mother's best friend. Several other Waxhaw boys attended Bethel Academy. Mrs. Howe rented out beds in her loft and meals to as many as half a dozen students at Bethel at one time. Andy was one of these students.

William Hill's Ironworks was about two miles down the road from the school. Though it had been burned by the British during the war, it was rebuilt and running again. Many trees were cut from the dense forests to fuel the furnaces. Wood smoke clouded the sky above the school and scented the air most hours of the day. Wares from the ironworks traveled in wagons along the road to Salisbury. There were andirons, Dutch ovens, kettles and many other items heading for merchant trade. William Hill often visited both Bethel Meeting House and Bethel Academy. His son, Billy Jr., around Jackson's age, may have studied there as well.

The war interrupted life for everyone, but especially the younger ones, who now needed to figure out where to go with their lives. These young people were now in their teens to late twenties. They had experienced fear, homelessness and loss during the war. An expensive education was not needed. They did need their own goals, drive and common sense to succeed. Bethel Academy and other such schools offered a jumping-off point to begin new lives as the adults they had become. With goals in mind and a good education as a foundation, they set down to study.

It is not known exactly how long Andy attended Bethel Academy, but he studied Latin and brushed up on many other subjects. He had the same goal as the other students. While he preferred riding over reading, he buckled down and gave his studies the same attention as horses, saddlery, socializing and gaming. He achieved his goal.

A few of Andy's classmates included Samuel Mayes, Billy Smith, James White Stephenson, William Cummins Davis, Robert Cunningham, Grizzel "Grizzy" McKenzie and Peggy Stinson. Billy and Andy had gone to school together at Waxhaw Academy. James was now in his late twenties. He was Andy's classmate and former teacher. William, a minister's nephew, was in his early twenties and also preparing for the ministry. Robert was from Mecklenburg County, which was near Charlotte. Tall and sociable, he was also in his early twenties. Grizzy and Peggy were the only two girls who were known to have attended. Grizzy's family was within walking distance. She was twenty-two years old. Peggy, age fourteen, came over from Fishing Creek. Andy was about sixteen or seventeen.

This school was more serious than any Andy had attended before. United in their goal to learn, the students had no use for classroom play. This was their job now. They socialized outside the classroom. After school was out and on weekends, they attended church and dances, went on picnics and participated in other events and fun excursions. When the students got together, they used their best manners as well as their best dress.

In later years, Andy remembered Dr. Allison, who was nineteen at this time, and Betsy Hill, Colonel Hill's oldest daughter, who was seventeen. They may have been students at the academy. Both were of Bethel's congregation. Their wedding would have been a major social event, celebrated with the same backcountry fun as at Andy's cousin Tommy Crawford's wedding a few years earlier. A lot had changed since that day when Andy was just a boy.

Andy is said to have dated—or courted, as it was known then—a few of the girls. Polly Massey is said to have been one who rejected him. Peggy Dickey was another one he may have dated. He may also have dated one of Major Crawford's daughters. As a widower in the White House, he sent her a silver snuffbox that he received after the Battle of New Orleans. Family myth has it that she had rejected him. Another story says Major Crawford put an end to their relationship. But those are just stories. The facts behind their true relationship are not known.

Andy may not have studied at Bethel long. He basically needed foundations in Latin and English to move on to the next level of studying law. He may have gone back and forth at times between Bethel Academy and the Waxhaws. During part of 1784, he stayed with either Major Crawford or the McCamies. While there, he earned money by teaching school for younger children. He taught at a school four miles north of Waxhaw Creek. The name of the school is unknown, lost to history. Andy's time there, though, is not. He had now gone beyond saddlery and gaming. He taught the children how to read and write. He kept classroom order, broke up fights and punished the children appropriately as needed. He was now, for the first time in his life, in a leadership role.

During 1784, Andy also helped Major Crawford, who was trying to settle Will Crawford's debts from the Galbraith incident. Major Crawford asked Andy to sell two of his slaves for him in Salisbury. He knew that Andy could ask Will's help if any legal issues came up. Andy traveled eighty miles north up the dusty Salisbury Road with

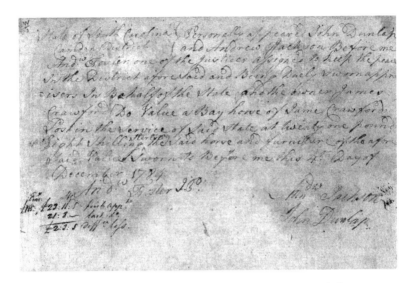

Andrew Jackson's appraisal of Jim Crawford's horse for military reimbursement after the Revolutionary War, December 4, 1784. *South Carolina Department of Archives & History.*

the slaves. After they were sold at market, he talked to Will about studying law. Will suggested moving to Salisbury, where there was not only a lot of legal business for experience and possible income but a lot of fun as well.

Some of Andy's relatives were very critical of the way he had squandered his small inheritance in Charleston. Nevertheless, Andy continued to think about how he could pay his expenses. His knowledge of horses was well respected, and one of his skills was horse appraisal. To earn money, in addition to teaching, he appraised horses for Revolutionary War claims. As an example, his cousin Jim Crawford lost a horse during the war. On December 4, 1784, Andy's appraisal of that horse was recorded in a legal document for Jim to receive reimbursement by the state.

Before Christmas, Andy was in Salisbury studying law with Spruce Macay (pronounced Macoy). He was slowly breaking his ties with the Waxhaws. Andy was seventeen years old.

Chapter 20
Lawyer Jackson

Approximately fifty families lived in Salisbury. Many of them, including Spruce Macay, were wealthy. Andy refused to be intimidated. He dressed according to his budget, often better than his budget allowed. He rode a good horse. He worked in a law office toward his goal of becoming a lawyer. Here, Andy achieved a social climb away from the ruggedness of the Waxhaws. Residents of Salisbury, though, would remember him as "the most roaring, rollicking, game-cocking, horse-racing, card-playing, mischievous fellow, that ever lived in Salisbury…the head of the rowdies hereabouts…more in the stable than in the office."[39]

In addition to the wealthy, residents of town included merchants, carpenters, tailors, blacksmiths, saddlers, tavern keepers and a silversmith. Streets were red mud. Wagons loaded with material goods and supplies kept the streets alive with activity. Andy still saw many people from the Waxhaws here since Salisbury was a county seat. One of the wagons was driven by Colonel Davie's brother Jo. He worked for William Hill at his ironworks, bringing in iron and iron products to sell, and would look after Hill's business interests while there.

At the top of the hill stood the Rowan County Courthouse, a twenty-by thirty-foot frame building. Nearby was the stone jail. Not far away were the stocks and the whipping post, accepted forms of colonial justice. Dunn's Mountain, a popular choice for an afternoon ride, was visible in the distance southeast of the courthouse. Not far from the courthouse, in between taverns and less imposing homes, stood a few mansions. Farther out lay plain log and frame houses and farms.

Many German-speaking immigrants lived southeast of Salisbury and knew little English. They referred to Salisbury as "Salzburg," perhaps to remind them of Austria. The familiar Ulster Irish lived to the north and the west.

Spruce Macay lived two blocks from the courthouse. His practice was in a small, fifteen- by sixteen-foot building next to but separate from his house. Always well dressed, he had dark hair and a dry sense of humor. He was thirty years old, and his wife, Fanny, was only three years older than Andy. She was beautiful, musical, smart and the daughter of Judge Richard Henderson.

Spruce Macay's law firm was the largest in Salisbury. Just as other law students did, Andy paid a fee to Macay to study with him. Under his direction, Andy copied legal documents by hand to learn their correct format. If a lawyer did not learn this exactly, he might damage his client's interests. In addition to copying legal documents over and over again, which could be rather boring, Andy was expected to read and memorize the law from books. Spruce Macay's professional library contained fifty-two law books that Andy would have studied. Macay, an experienced lawyer, was there to help when the interpretation of a passage of law was unclear. Macay had also served as the state's attorney since 1779. The experience Andy would gain in Salisbury would soon change his life and eventually the course of United States history forever.

One of the classic law books Andy studied was the four-volume *Commentaries on the Laws of England* by William Blackstone. Another valuable resource to Andy was *Abridgment of the Law* by Matthew Bacon. Between these two resources alone, he learned the meaning of Latin legal phrases and how to interpret court cases based on previous real-court examples. He studied many more law books than these two, but he memorized these two resources in particular forward and backward. In fact, it is said that as a circuit lawyer, Andy carried his own copy of Bacon's *Abridgment* wrapped in buckskin in his saddlebag as he traveled. Other lawyers made fun of him because he "cited it constantly."[40] The day would come, though, when they would not make fun of him for working hard on his studies. The presidency would one day be his.

Macay's office had a fireplace, chairs and at least two large writing desks for the clerks. The one Andy used was made of white pine and walnut with a slanted, hinged top. The walls were covered with shelves of law books. When Andy was not copying legal documents for Macay, he was reading from these books and copying passages for his own use in a future practice of his own.

William Cupples was also a clerk studying with Macay at this time. He likely sat at the other writing desk in Macay's office near Andy. William was a local boy who had already been there about a year when Andy arrived. They became good friends.

Evidence suggests that Andy did not study law continuously in Salisbury in 1785, but he was certainly learning the law. He needed income, so he took legal work when he could get it for both the experience and the money. As he mastered legal language and created his own legal documents, his self-confidence as a soon-to-be lawyer grew.

Andy's friend John McNairy, from his time in Guilford, had also studied with Macay. John's practice and permanent home was near Guilford, but he traveled the circuit as a lawyer. This meant he traveled to different courthouses in different counties to conduct business. Salisbury was the Rowan County seat, so much of his business was at the Salisbury courthouse. Some circuit lawyers, because they traveled so much, often reserved rooms in different towns so they would always have a place to stay. This was the case with McNairy in Salisbury.

Andy's cousin Will Crawford also studied with Macay at the same time as McNairy. Now, Will was also a Salisbury lawyer. Both John and Will began their law practices in May 1784. Before Andy arrived, they were probably roommates during this time.

Andy studied with Macay for about two years. John McNairy, Will Crawford and Andy roomed together at Rowan House, a tavern about a block down from the courthouse. Joseph Hughes ran it as one of the best taverns in town. In each room was a bed with a feather mattress, a mirror and a chamber pot. They did not have indoor plumbing. They used an outhouse instead. In the curtained dining room, they ate off pewter plates on cloth-covered tables. In the attached bar area, guests, including Andy, gathered for talk, drink, dance, smoking and planning practical jokes. One instance involved stealing the gates from houses. While they thought this was hilarious, the homeowners did not.

At this time, smoking was a leisurely habit practiced while men sat by the fire and talked or when they played cards. Like most young men of the backcountry, Jackson smoked. He probably learned it at an early age. Purchasing his tobacco at the local store in twists of tobacco leaves, he shredded the leaves before packing them into a long clay pipe.

During this time, Andy, John and Will developed a bit of a reputation for their pranks, card games, horse races and general rowdiness around town. They were known as the "Inseparables." Andy was in his late teens, while John and Will were in their mid-twenties.

Once, Andy, Will and John decided to have a few friends over to their room for a party. Of course, they were drinking. The room was small. The more they drank, the rowdier the crowd got. Glasses were smashed, tables and chairs were broken and so on before they tore up the bedding and curtains. Finally, they threw the remaining alcohol onto the fire, resulting in a burst of flames. While they finally put out the flames, this little party cost them quite a bit and added to their wild reputation in town.

Other incidents happened accidentally at Rowan House. Judy, a twelve-year-old house slave working at the tavern, was straightening the Inseparables' room while the men were downstairs in the dining room. Andy, John and Will had just returned from a hunting trip, so the room was scattered with their guns, clothes and probably books as well. Judy was curious. She picked up one of the guns to get a closer look and turned it over and around to check it out. BANG! The gun went off as buckshot soared into the ceiling. Judy's eyes must have gotten large with fright as she gasped and dropped the gun. Downstairs must have been a commotion, as people ran upstairs to see what had happened. Judy was scared but quick. She ran out of the room and hid before anyone returned.

Andy was competitive and attracted competitive challenges, often with laughter involved. Wealthy Hugh Montgomery Jr., in his twenties with a bit of extra weight on him compared to rail-thin Andy, bet Andy that he could beat him in a foot race. To sweeten the deal, Montgomery offered to carry another man on his back for a head start. Everyone standing around laughed at this. Andy accepted the challenge even though all knew what the outcome would be. They just wanted a bit of fun. The crowd moved to the horse race track north of town.

The race began with shouts and clapping from the crowd. With another man perched on his back, determined Montgomery held onto him tight as he ran, probably swaying a bit with the extra passenger. After about an eighth of a mile, Andy took off down the track with his long legs flying. More shouts, laughter and clapping from the crowd urged them both to run faster. The crowd hurrahed and laughed as Andy crossed the finish line first, winning, surprisingly, by only two or three yards. They all had a good time, and Andy won money in a bet.

Court week was a social event as well as an economic boost for the town. Six times a year, lawyers and their clients, businessmen, slave dealers and horse traders came to Salisbury on business from all over the backcountry. Outside the courthouse, men traded horses, played games, conducted business and fought bare-fisted style.

Andy, John and Will tied their horses to the hitching posts outside John Steele's store. Andy purchased a quire, or twenty-four sheets, of paper. This was a standard purchase for a law student. The next day, probably to look good in court, John and Will purchased new shoes.

Just reading and copying documents would not give Andy or any other clerk the full knowledge needed to pass the bar examination and be a successful lawyer. Courtroom observation was also necessary. In this way, the student saw the application of his studies in action by licensed lawyers and judges. Attendance at court sessions also provided opportunities to meet future clients, as well as to size up legal competition. According to historian Henrik Booraem, "In Salisbury, the County Court of Pleas and Quarter Sessions met every three months, in February, May, August, and

November. North Carolina's highest court, the Superior Court, which traveled from one district to another, met for ten-day terms at Salisbury beginning 15 March and 15 September."[41]

Andy observed the way Macay and other lawyers interviewed witnesses, as well as the way they gathered evidence for a case. William R. Davie argued in the Superior Court. Andy would also have observed his military hero here in action as a lawyer.

In 1785, Robert Ellison, a wealthy man from the backcountry, sued Will Crawford in Salisbury for £261, six shillings fourpence. Apparently, the incident at Major Crawford's public station had caught up with him. Ellison hired lawyer Billy Sharpe, while Will hired McNairy, Stokes and William Tatham. The case came to jury trial in August 1787. Will lost. This was a tremendous financial burden for him and may have influenced his decision to leave Salisbury around this time.

How did Andy afford to pay for his time in Salisbury? He had to pay for his tailored clothes, tobacco, drink, fees to Macay, paper for his studies, room, basic supplies, meals, pastimes like horse racing and antics like the party at Rowan House. He did some legal work on the side, but that would not have supplied enough funds for three years in Salisbury. Major Crawford did not help him or Will financially. Even if Andy received rent money from his parents' land, which was being managed by Jim Crawford for him, that would not have been enough to support himself the entire time. History is unclear on this point, but other biographers guess that he raised money through gambling. Biographer Marquis James suggests that Andy "gambled not always as a sportsman who can afford to lose, but as an adventurer who has to win."[42]

One witness claims that Andy paid off his store account by winning card game bets from merchant Hughes. A popular card game at this time that Andy probably played with Hughes was All Fours. It had a couple of other names, including Seven-up and Old Sledge. In All Fours, each player is dealt six cards. A trump card is turned up in the middle. There are four suits in a deck of cards: diamonds, hearts, spades and clubs. The trump suit is above the others and can capture even high cards in another suit. The players holding the high trump and the low trump automatically score one point each. Other points can be scored. Whichever player scores seven points first wins the game. This card game did not have to be played as a gambling game for money, but Andy and his friends usually did. While Andy may have won some money this way, he played cards mostly for the fun of it. Card games were a popular southern frontier pastime.

Andy also made money with cockfights. Cockfighting was and is a cruel game that hurts, maims and kills the roosters involved. In Andy's time, it was considered a popular and acceptable sport and not just on the frontier. Cockfighting was also a gentleman's game in Britain, attended by members of the aristocracy. Andy grew up with this sport and was good enough at training the birds to win money at it.

At the end of Andy's second year in Salisbury, Eleanor Faust and Andy signed up with a dancing school conducted by a traveling dance instructor. Eleanor was the wife of German tradesman Peter Faust. She was also the older sister of George Dunn, one of Andy's wild friends. For a fee, this dance master taught dance, critiqued dance styles and held a series of balls as practice and a final one as proof of students' dance skills. Andy became one of the managers of a Christmas ball to be held in the courthouse. What did Andy do as manager of the ball? He created the guest list, sent out the invitations, hired the musicians and provided refreshments.

Andy thought it would be fun to invite Molly and Rachel Wood, a less than respectable mother and daughter in town. They were not considered part of this society crowd of which Andy was now a member. Though he had a lot of adult responsibility, Andy was still very young. He may have thought this would be a funny prank, but he did not consider the feelings of others.

Andy probably hand-delivered Molly's and Rachel's invitations. They came to the ball in inappropriate dresses. All eyes were upon them as the whispers of gossip began and the room buzzed with confusion. The other managers stopped the dance. Molly and Rachel were asked to leave. They did not understand why they had been invited if they were to be treated this way. Andy went after them to smooth things over. He had wanted to see what would happen, and he did—at the expense of Molly and Rachel.

Andy was snubbed by the women in town. Ellen Faust did not change her mind about him for the rest of her life. Fanny, Spruce Macay's wife, may have been among these women. If so, it would explain why Andy decided to leave his studies with Macay and sign on with Colonel John Stokes, a thirty-one-year-old brilliant North Carolina lawyer in Montgomery County who also had a practice in Salisbury. William Cupples also left Macay around this same time and went to study with Stokes.

Back in May 1780, Colonel Stokes had been caught up in Tarleton's massacre at Buford's Defeat in the Waxhaws. He was taken with the wounded to the Waxhaw Meeting House and may have been cared for by Betty Jackson. Severely wounded, he had a scarred gash reaching from his forehead across his eye, with other scars on his face. He was missing his left forefinger. His right hand was now a silver knob. His assistant, a free mulatto named Roger Stapleton, helped care for him. Stokes, known for his sense of humor and kindness, did not let his war wounds hold him back. He established his law practice in Salisbury in 1784. From Colonel Stokes, Andy and William learned the value of courtroom dramatics. Using his new hand to his advantage, Stokes tapped the knob on the table to emphasize his point in court. It rang like a bell.

Just like Andy, Stokes loved horses. Stokes was not married at this time. By 1788, he would marry Elizabeth Pearson, an heiress. They would build a mansion on the Yadkin together. For now, he lived on the family farm in Montgomery County with his younger brother Montfort (pronounced Mumford). Montfort was in his mid-twenties, just a few years older than Andy, and had recently received his law license. Montfort, too, served in the war and was on one of the prison ships similar to the ones Andy's cousins were on. William Cupples, Montfort and Andy all enjoyed cards as well. They were all still a bit wild, but they were friends.

Stokes was more of a circuit lawyer who traveled around Salisbury District, while Macay was more grounded within the city of Salisbury. Salisbury District covered a large part of North Carolina from the boundary of Virginia to the north to South Carolina to the south. Stokes took Andy and Cupples out of the city and onto the trail.

In 1787, John Stokes was elected to the Constitutional Convention in Philadelphia. William R. Davie and Alexander Martin, governor of North Carolina and John McNairy's family's neighbor, also attended. The convention met in May to draw up a new Constitution for the United States. Little did any of them know then that young Andy Jackson would one day lead this newly independent nation.

Horses were a passion for Andy and racing them even more so. Winning money on bets he placed with horses—and he did own some of his own—was likely a primary source of income at this time in his life. A horse entered in a race was evaluated by the age and size of the animal. Andy served as a consultant to others to assess the condition and merit of a horse's suitability for racing. Establishing himself as an expert on horses, he knew how to make money with that expertise from horse appraisals to racing. Throughout the rest of his life, Andy's love of horses would continue.

A warrant issued in August 1787 indicates a horse race gone wrong. The warrant was for the arrest of Andy and two of his friends, Hugh Montgomery Jr. and William Cupples. Accused of trespass, a broad term with a variety of legal definitions, Andrew Baird and John Ludlow sought money to pay for damages by Andy and his friends. While we do not know the specifics, it appears that Ludlow raced his Thoroughbred horse, Young Whirligig, against one of Andy's or one owned by Andy, Montgomery and Cupples together. Baird, a farmer, and Ludlow, a horse breeder from New Jersey, asked £500 as payment for damages. That would be the cost of an expensive racehorse. Two men from Salisbury helped the trio make bond. Daniel Clary, a tavern keeper, and Henry Giles, a wealthy gentleman with an interest in horse racing, paid £1,000 to keep them out of jail. Giles was married to Elizabeth, another sister of George Dunn, one of Andy's wild friends. The case was settled out of court, but it supports Andy's interest in horse racing and tells of the support of Andy's friends in Salisbury.

Montfort Stokes, William Cupples, William R. Davie and many others around Andy were Masons. Masons were and are a secret society of men with good character. They stressed virtue and kindness in their actions and were obligated to help one another. Andy grew up familiar with the Masonic Order in the Waxhaws.

Men involved in Masonry were educated community leaders. At their lodge meetings, drunkenness, obscenities and abusive language were forbidden, as were arguments about politics and religion. They got together for conversation, smoking and drinking in moderation. These men were not the rowdy crowd Andy was used to associating with. His new friends exposed him to the inner life of the Masonic Order. It is not known exactly when Andy joined as a Mason, but in later life, he was a devoted and active member. These new friends set examples for new behavior and planted the seeds within him for future goals.

After six months with Colonel Stokes and after passing his oral exam given by Judges Samuel Ashe and John F. Williams, Andy was admitted to the bar on September 26, 1787. Andy's friend William Cupples was also admitted to the bar at this time.

Talking and socializing came naturally to Andy. These traits would prove to be assets to him in his law career. He would frequently stand around to talk outside the courthouses he visited as a circuit lawyer. Standing over six feet tall, he had rod-straight posture. His blue eyes were set in a narrow face with a long jaw line. He kept his light brown hair tied back and covered with a hat. His clothes were made by a local tailor. Below his long coat, he wore a dark or striped waistcoat over a ruffled linen shirt. Knee breeches and stockings covered his legs, while buckled shoes covered his feet.

Andy remembered his days in Salisbury later in life: "Ah, I was a raw lad then, but I did my best."[43]

Chapter 21
Onward and Westward

A ndy was now a circuit lawyer. It was cheaper to be licensed to practice in county court than Superior Court. Andy and William chose to be licensed only in the county courts for now. When they had more experience and more money, their goal was to obtain their licenses to practice in the Superior Court as well.

Within Salisbury District were eight counties, each with its own county court. These courts handled small civil suits. Cases involving murder, horse stealing and other serious charges were heard in Superior Court twice a year in Salisbury. Superior Court cases were high drama. Only in Superior Court could a convicted criminal be branded on the cheeks as a horse thief with an H and a T. Only in Superior Court could a convicted criminal have his ears cut off. County court judges were only able to punish convicted criminals with fines or whippings or by placing them in the stocks. This was the court where Andy practiced. This was the court where Andy sometimes protected his clients, but sometimes he lost cases as well.

Each county court met once in a quarter during a week assigned by the state legislature. These were known as quarter sessions. Every county was assigned a different court week. Weeks were assigned consecutively to adjoining counties. A circuit lawyer, if he wanted the business, could plan well and attend them all. Andy and William

Cupples rode the entire circuit. They wanted the professional experience as well as the increased income.

It took four hundred miles and eight weeks to ride the circuit. The roads were terrible. The forests were dense. The terrain covered included mountains and sand hills. The rivers were sometimes flooded, making crossing dangerous. It is likely that Will Crawford and John McNairy practiced in all eight counties as well. Often these men traveled in groups between counties, as they were all attending the same court sessions on established dates. Lawyers who did not travel the entire circuit would join them for part of the journey. They also traveled with their slaves or free men like Stokes's Roger Stapleton, who helped take care of him.

As they traveled between court sessions, they gambled and socialized, joked around and kidded one another. Occasionally, talk veered toward court cases and politics. Sometimes they carried racehorses with them for entertainment. Sometimes they ended up with livestock as payment, which also traveled with them. They would stop at log taverns along the way for overnight shelter. While there, they might gain more business or maybe just a friendly game of cards. Traveling as a group this way passed the time more quickly on the circuit. Andy traveled the circuit for about six months.

At this time, North Carolina's border reached to the Mississippi River. Much of the western part of the state was unexplored. About 180 miles beyond the settled part of North Carolina was the Western District, what would one day become the state of Tennessee. Andy had his eye on this land. Like his parents before him when they left Ireland for America in search of new opportunities, Andy sought not only opportunity but adventure as well.

Andy's friend John McNairy was elected to the judgeship of Davidson County in the newly created Superior Court of the Western District. He was appointed in December 1787. It was too dangerous to travel in wintertime to cross mountains unless it was an emergency. There were rough roads, rivers, slopes of bare rock and wild animals such as wolves and bears, just to name a few of the obstacles. Once over the mountains, there was another two hundred miles to cross before reaching Davidson County. McNairy asked a few people to travel with him, including Andy. Will Crawford

Andrew Jackson
equestrian statue in
Lafayette Square,
Washington, D.C.
*Wikimedia Commons, photo
by dbKing.*

was not asked. One of the reasons may have been Will's drinking problem. Regardless, Will was like a brother to Andy, and it must have been hard to leave him behind.

Before leaving for Davidson County, Andy paid off his debts in Salisbury. Those included John Steele's store, as well as the remaining bills at Rowan House. Near the end of March 1788, Andy left the Carolinas, never to return. He was twenty-one years old. McNairy would eventually appoint Jackson as the attorney general or public prosecutor for Davidson County. While Andy had already lived a lifetime in his young years, he had many more adventures in front of him. This was just the beginning.

Glossary

affliction: the cause of persistent pain or distress; great suffering

anguished: tormented

exult: to be extremely joyful

forge: to form by heating or hammering

Loyalist: a supporter of the king

militia: armed forces of a country subject to call only in an emergency

morale: mental and emotional condition of an individual or group

Patriot: someone who is against the king

perseverance: continuation beyond a certain point or to an exceptional degree

quarter: not killing a defeated enemy

reputation: recognition by others for overall quality or character

saddletree: the frame of a saddle

skirmish: a minor fight in the war

stalemate: no possible move; a draw; deadlock

topography: natural and man-made features of a place

Tory: a supporter of the king

Whig: someone who is against the king

Notes

Chapter 3

1. Catawba Indian Nation.

Chapter 4

2. *Documents Relating to the Birthplace*, 87.
3. Ibid.
4. Parton, *Life of Andrew Jackson*, 64.

Chapter 8

5. Booraem, *Young Hickory*, 28.

Chapter 9

6. Kirk, interview.
7. James, *Life of Andrew Jackson*, 20.

Chapter 10

8. National Archives and Records Administration.
9. Fodor's, *Fodor's Ireland 2014*, 618.
10. Hakim, *From Colonies to Country*, 144.
11. Berkin, *Revolutionary Mothers*, 143.

Chapter 11

12. Smith and Owsley, *Papers of Andrew Jackson*, 5.
13. Meacham, *American Lion*, 11.
14. Booraem, *Young Hickory*, 52.

Chapter 12

15. Ibid., 67.
16. Ibid.

Chapter 13

17. Pettus, *Waxhaws*, 39.
18. Booraem, *Young Hickory*, 83.

Chapter 14

19. Alderman, *One Heroic Hour at King's Mountain*, 19.
20. Messick, *King's Mountain*, 91.
21. Draper, *King's Mountain*, 509.
22. Alderman, *One Heroic Hour at King's Mountain*, 34.
23. Messick, *King's Mountain*, 135.
24. Cobb, *American Battlefields*, 79.
25. Messick, *King's Mountain*, 142.
26. Ibid., 145.
27. Draper, *King's Mountain*, 584.
28. Messick, *King's Mountain*, 147.
29. Ibid., 150.
30. Ibid., 151.
31. Alderman, *One Heroic Hour at King's Mountain*, 53.

Chapter 15

32. Booraem, *Young Hickory*, 93.
33. Alderman, *Overmountain Men*, 130.

Chapter 17

34. Booraem, *Young Hickory*, 108.

Chapter 18

35. Ibid., 116.
36. Smith and Owsley, *Papers of Andrew Jackson*, 7.
37. Ibid.

Chapter 19

38. Ibid.

Chapter 20

39. James, *Life of Andrew Jackson*, 34–35.
40. Booraem, *Young Hickory*, 171.
41. Ibid., 172.
42. James, *Life of Andrew Jackson*, 38.
43. Parton, *Life of Andrew Jackson*, 108.

Bibliography

Alderman, Pat. *One Heroic Hour at King's Mountain.* Erwin, TN: Erwin Publishing Co., Inc., 1968.

————. *The Overmountain Men: Battle of King's Mountain, Cumberland Decade, State of Franklin, Southwest Territory.* Johnson City, TN: Overmountain Press, 1986.

Allison, Robert J., ed. *The Boston Tea Party (New England Remembers Series).* Beverly, MA: Commonwealth Editions, 2007.

Bass, Robert D. *Gamecock: The Life and Campaigns of General Thomas Sumter.* New York: Holt, Rinehart, and Winston, 1961.

Berkin, Carol. *Revolutionary Mothers: Women in the Struggle for America's Independence.* New York: Alfred A. Knopf, 2005.

Booraem, Hendrik. *Young Hickory: The Making of Andrew Jackson.* Dallas, TX: Taylor Trade Publishing, 2001.

Catawba Indian Nation. catawbaindian.net/about-us/early-history. Accessed December 29, 2013.

Cobb, Hubbard. *American Battlefields: A Complete Guide to the Historic Conflicts in Words, Maps, and Photos.* New York: Macmillan, 1995.

Cockrell, Michael R. *The Battle of Hanging Rock: August 6, 1780.* Winnsboro, SC: Two Bullet Publishers, 2009.

Documents Relating to the Birthplace of Andrew Jackson: Selections Taken from Walter Clark MSS. Vol. 3, 240, 312–32. Microfilm. Charlotte-Mecklenburg Public Library.

Drake, Francis S. *Tea Leaves: Being a Collection of Letters and Documents Relating to the Shipment of Tea to the American Colonies in the Year 1773, by the East India Tea Company*. Detroit, MI: Singing Tree Press, 1970.

Draper, Lyman C. *King's Mountain and Its Heroes: History of the Battle of King's Mountain, October 7th, 1780, and the Events Which Led to It*. Baltimore, MD: Genealogical Publishing Co., Inc., 1971.

Edwards, Roberta. *Who Was George Washington?* New York: Grosset & Dunlap, 2009.

Fodor's. *Fodor's Ireland 2014*. New York: Fodor's Travel, 2014.

Griswold, Wesley S. *The Night the Revolution Began: The Boston Tea Party, 1773*. Brattleboro, VT: Stephen Greene Press, 1972.

Hakim, Joy. *From Colonies to Country: 1710–1791*. Book 3, 2nd edition (*A History of Us*). New York: Oxford University Press, 1999.

Historic Brattonsville. Battle of Huck's Defeat. chmuseums.org/battle-of-hucks-defeat-hb. Accessed February 22, 2014.

James, Marquis. *The Life of Andrew Jackson*. Vol. 1: *Border Captain*. New York: Bobbs-Merrill Company, 1938.

Kirk, Jennifer, historical interpreter at Mansker's Station, Goodlettsville, TN. Interview, November 23, 2013.

Lewis, Kenneth E. "Economic Development in the South Carolina Backcountry: A View from Camden." In *The Southern Colonial Backcountry: Interdisciplinary Perspectives on Frontier Communities*, edited by David Colin Crass, Steven D. Smith, Martha A. Zierden and Richard D. Brooks, 87–117. Knoxville: University of Tennessee Press, 1998.

Meacham, Jon. *American Lion: Andrew Jackson in the White House*. New York: Random House, 2008.

Messick, Hank. *King's Mountain: The Epic of the Blue Ridge "Mountain Men" in the American Revolution*. Boston: Little, Brown and Company, 1976.

National Archives and Records Administration. www.archives.gov/exhibits/charters/declaration_transcript.html. Accessed February 21, 2014.

National Park Service, Fort Moultrie. www.nps.gov/fosu/historyculture/fort_moultrie.htm. Accessed February 21, 2014.

Old Salem. MESDA Craftsman Database. William Hill Ironworks. Accessed November 5, 2013.

Parton, James. *A Life of Andrew Jackson.* Vol. 1. New York: Mason Brothers, 1860.

Pedigree Online Thoroughbred Database. www.pedigreequery.com/flimnap. Accessed December 7, 2013.

Pettus, Louise. *The Waxhaws.* Rock Hill, SC: privately printed, 1993.

Piecuch, Jim. *The Blood Be Upon Your Head: Tarleton and the Myth of Buford's Massacre: The Battle of the Waxhaws, May 29, 1780.* Lugoff, SC: Southern Campaigns of the American Revolution Press, 2010.

Ramsay, David, MD. *Ramsay's History of South Carolina from Its First Settlement in 1670 to the Year 1808.* Newberry, SC: W.J. Duffie, 1858.

Robinson, Blackwell P. *The Revolutionary War Sketches of William R. Davie.* Raleigh: North Carolina Division of Archives and History, 1976.

Savas, Theodore P., and J. David Dameron. *A Guide to the Battles of the American Revolution.* New York: Savas Beatie, 2006.

Smith, Sam B., and Harriet Chappell Owsley, eds. *The Papers of Andrew Jackson.* Vol. 1: *1770–1803.* Knoxville: University of Tennessee Press, 1980.

Thorp, Daniel B. "Taverns and Communities: The Case of Rowan County, North Carolina." In *The Southern Colonial Backcountry: Interdisciplinary Perspectives on Frontier Communities,* edited by David Colin Crass, Steven D. Smith, Martha A. Zierden and Richard D. Brooks, 76–86. Knoxville: University of Tennessee Press, 1998.

Young, Alfred F. *The Shoemaker and the Tea Party.* Boston: Beacon Press, 1999.

About the Author

J ennifer Hunsicker has worked in libraries for twenty years. She has degrees in history and library science and is working toward her MFA in writing through Spalding University, specializing in writing for children and young adults. She is a member of the Society of Children's Book Writers and Illustrators, as well as Biographers International. With a love of research and needle arts, she lives in Tennessee with her vivid imagination. This is her first book.